T0080862

# MENDING THE

# Soul

## STUDENT EDITION

Understanding and

Healing Abuse

Steven R. Tracy, ThM, PhD
and Celestia G. Tracy, MA, LPC

with Kristi Ickes Garrison, MSW, LCSW

# MENDING THE
# SOul
## STUDENT EDITION

Understanding and

Healing Abuse

youth
specialties

ZONDERVAN

*Mending the Soul Student Edition*
Copyright © 2011 by Steven R. Tracy and Celestia G. Tracy

YS Youth Specialties is a trademark of YOUTHWORKS!, INCORPORATED and is registered with the United States Patent and Trademark Office.

This title is also available as a Zondervan ebook.
Visit www.zondervan.com/ebooks.

This title is also available in a Zondervan audio edition.
Visit www.zondervan.fm.

Requests for information should be addressed to:

Zondervan, *Grand Rapids, Michigan 49530*

---

Library of Congress Cataloging-in-Publication Data

Tracy, Steven R.
        Mending the Soul / Steven R. Tracy and Celestia G. Tracy with Kristi Ickes Garrison.
    — Student Edition
            p.    cm.
        Includes bibliographical references (p.        ) and index.
        ISBN  978-0-310-67143-5 (softcover : alk. paper)  1.  Christian teenagers—Religious life. 2.
    Abused teenagers—Religious life.  I. Tracy, Celestia G., 1958- II. Garrison, Kristi Iches. III. Title.
    BV4531.3.T73 2011
    248.8'627 — dc23                                                                                    2011028132

---

All Scripture quotations, unless otherwise indicated, are taken from the Holy Bible, *New International Version®, NIV®.* Copyright © 1973, 1978, 1984, 2011 by Biblica, Inc.™ Used by permission of Zondervan. All rights reserved worldwide.

Any Internet addresses (websites, blogs, etc.) and telephone numbers in this book are offered as a resource. They are not intended in any way to be or imply an endorsement by Zondervan, nor does Zondervan vouch for the content of these sites and numbers for the life of this book.

All rights reserved. No part of this publication may be reproduced, stored in a retrieval system, or transmitted in any form or by any means—electronic, mechanical, photocopy, recording, or any other—except for brief quotations in printed reviews, without the prior permission of the publisher.

Cover design: Lucas Art and Design
Cover photo: Masterfile
Interior design: David Conn

*Printed in the United States of America*

---

11  12  13  14  15  16  /DCI/  22  21  20  19  18  17  16  15  14  13  12  11  10  9  8  7  6  5  4  3  2  1

# SPECIAL THANKS

We would like to thank Kristi Ickes Garrison for her dedication to the thousands of students who have been blessed enough to come under her care. She's a tireless and passionate advocate for teens everywhere, and she lives to help the adults in their lives understand and love them well. In many ways, she has been a pioneer in taking to hurting students the message of hope and healing from abuse.

Kristi came to us several years ago and asked about resources like *Mending the Soul* for adolescents in our public schools. She described support groups offered for teen moms, addicts, and for teens who needed to learn anger management skills; but it was clear to her (and to us) that the pain of abuse and neglect was the source that drove many of these problematic behaviors. At the time, we didn't know of many resources on abuse and healing, so Kristi took the theology, research, and healing model of *Mending the Soul* and packaged it for students in public schools. She writes with the same authenticity and passion with which she speaks.

We've enjoyed working together on this project. May you, the reader, be blessed and supported by the theology of abuse and healing, and the practical resources you'll find within these pages. Thank you, Kristi, for loving God and students like you do.

– Steve and Celestia, June 2010

# CONTENTS

# PREFACE

Dear Student,

I'm so thankful you decided to pick up this book. You may be reading this
because an adult you trust gave it to you, or you might have borrowed
it from a friend. The way you found it doesn't matter—it's just important
that you did. Within these pages you'll learn three things. First, we all
have pain in our lives; second, your attitudes and actions will reflect your
pain; and third, no matter how much you've been through, you can find
healing and freedom.

I want to challenge you up front: First, don't quit reading this book.
There's not going to be a test—you're not getting a grade. This isn't
school. This is real-life stuff and it's important. Even if you read things
that don't apply to you, I guarantee you'll read something that applies to
a friend's situation. When reading something that's painful, keep going.
You have this book at this time in your life for a reason.

Second, actively engage in this book. At the end of each chapter,
you'll find some questions to answer. There's some space for you to begin
answering there, but we encourage you to get a journal or notebook
where you can record more of your thoughts and feelings. You'll see three
levels of questions. Each level goes a little deeper, and you can decide
how much you want to do. You might not feel able to do everything now,
but you may decide to come back later. Just do what you can when you're
ready. Healing is a process!

Third, get connected. Find a friend or adult who you can talk to about
what you're reading. You were hurt in the context of relationship, and
you'll be healed in the context of relationship as well. I promise that if
you don't quit and you get connected, you'll see some amazing things
happen in your life.

I'm so proud of your willingness to take this journey. Through these pages you'll read story after story about other teens and young adults who've taken this journey as well. Believe them and believe me: The healing is worth it!

– Kristi Ickes Garrison

# NOTE TO THE READER

*Mending the Soul—Student Edition* is an adaptation and condensation of models, research, and application exercises found in *Mending the Soul: Understanding and Healing Abuse* (Zondervan, 2005) by Steven R. Tracy, and *Mending the Soul Workbook*, 3rd ed. (Mending the Soul Ministries, 2009) by Celestia G. Tracy. For a more in-depth development of the concepts and exercises found in the *Student Edition*, please refer to these two works.

The stories and examples used in this book are based on actual events, but various details have been changed to preserve the anonymity of the individuals involved. The information in this book shouldn't be construed as professional or legal counsel. Readers are encouraged to consult legal and medical professionals with specific questions or concerns.

This book contains references to some popular songs as examples of the principles discussed:

"Family Portrait" by P!nk
"I'm OK" by Christina Aguilera
"Because of You" by Kelly Clarkson
"Easier to Run" by Linkin Park
"Healing Begins" by Tenth Avenue North
"Jesus of Suburbia" by Green Day

# INTRODUCTION

God created us to be alive and complete in him. We're designed to know what we feel and need in order to express those things to the people who love us. We're created to trust, share our hurts, and be dependent on others as we walk through life. We're meant to be open and transparent with God, so he can work in and through us to bring hope to the world.

In the biblical creation account, we're told that God created humans to experience closeness with him and with each other—we're meant to enjoy perfect community, with freedom to be ourselves without judgment, criticism, or condemnation.

So, what happened? Instead of this ideal, we have a world of fear and pain. We get hurt and hurt others in return. As a result of this pain, we feel that we can't trust God because he "allowed us to get hurt." We avoid relationships with other people because we don't want to get hurt again. And we use anything we can think of to escape and try to feel better.

In this book we're going to talk about some of the most painful disruptions in God's design for our lives—pain in the form of abuse and abandonment. Among these and the other themes of this book, we're going to be talking about some tough stuff. But first, we must understand where abuse comes from and what happened to God's original design.

It shouldn't be surprising to learn that there's so much pain in our society. We hurt one another because we're all born with an internal pull toward sin. Sin is anything less than perfection—it's anything that falls short of a perfect attitude and perfect actions 100 percent of the time. It's anything that misses the mark of God's standard. In basketball, only a shot that makes it all the way into the net scores points. It doesn't matter if you miss the shot by a lot or if it hits the rim and bounces out—if it's not perfect, it doesn't count. Sin is the same way. All of us fall short of God's perfect character in various ways.

Human sinfulness is expressed in countless hurtful ways: selfishly meeting one's own needs at the expense of others, insulting others to build oneself up, telling vicious lies, physically assaulting others—we could go on and on. These become (and are) the characteristics of unhealthy or abusive people and unhealthy or abusive families. Abuse is the result of sin. Abuse is universally present in every culture because sin is universal. The Bible tells us,

> ... Jews and Gentiles alike are all under sin. As it is written:
> "There is no one righteous, not even one;
> there is no one who understands;
> there is no one who seeks God.
> All have turned away,
> they have together become worthless;
> there is no one who does good,
> not even one."
> "Their throats are open graves;
> their tongues practice deceit."
> "The poison of vipers is on their lips."
> "Their mouths are full of cursing and bitterness."
> "Their feet are swift to shed blood;
> ruin and misery mark their ways,
> and the way of peace they do not know."
> "There is no fear of God before their eyes" (Romans 3:9–18).[1]

This passage teaches that we all have an internal pull toward sin and when sin overtakes us, we can become abusive in our words and actions, and we can damage one another. The effects from that damage are carried with us every day.

Your pain needs to be healed so you can live the life God meant for you to live in the first place. This book will address how to identify and heal inner wounds.

## There's Hope!

The good news is that even though sin, abuse, and pain are all devastating to God's perfect design for your life, there's hope! We've met with students who come from the most horrific of abuse situations who're able to thrive and succeed. We know students who were addicted, abandoned, and alone who've been able to break those destructive patterns. By making changes in their lives, these students also positively affect their families for generations to come.

Throughout this book we'll address abuse and healing from a Christian perspective. That can be difficult because when you experience deep pain, it's normal to question your faith and wonder if God really cares. In fact, one of the first things to get damaged by abuse is how a person sees God. Therefore, we hope to correct some of the hurtful ways that pain and even religion can distort the reality of God's love and good character.

We'll do our best to be respectful and give you some key points to think over. We encourage you to consider how these points apply to your life. For some of you, they will. Others may have more questions—and that's okay. All of us have questions and doubts. It's good to be honest about the questions and doubts you have, talk about them with others you trust, and ultimately make your faith your own.

God knows everything—that characteristic is called *omniscience*. And since God knows everything, he also knows and sees all of the pain and abuse you've experienced and the struggles you're facing right now. However, just because God *sees* it, doesn't mean he's *okay* with it. Please don't confuse God's *awareness* with his *approval*. In fact, God *hates* abuse and the pain it causes. It's his promise to take what's horrifying and turn it around to use for good.

THE LORD EXAMINES THE RIGHTEOUS,
BUT THE WICKED, THOSE WHO LOVE VIOLENCE,
HE HATES WITH A PASSION....
FOR THE LORD IS RIGHTEOUS,
HE LOVES JUSTICE;
THE UPRIGHT WILL SEE HIS FACE. (PSALM 11:5, 7)

In the first century, the most abusive and cruel method of death was crucifixion. The purpose of crucifixion was to humiliate and torture criminals publicly. It's fascinating that Jesus, the center point of the Christian faith, was put to death by crucifixion, yet today, a cross has become the symbol of his followers. Crosses are even worn as jewelry. That doesn't make sense—why would people wear a torture device around their necks?

This demonstrates a miracle! The cross is a beautiful example of something horribly abusive being transformed into something beautiful. In fact we can't think of another example of such a transformation. Only God is capable of taking something ugly and horrifying and turning it into one of the most respected and recognized symbols of faith, hope, and peace in the world. When Christians see a cross, we don't see torture and death—we see love, hope, and strength. The same miracle is possible with our lives! Welcome to God's journey of healing and transformation. We're so glad you're here!

# PART ONE

# Figuring Out Your Pain

MAY THE PAIN YOU HAVE KNOWN
AND THE CONFLICT YOU HAVE
EXPERIENCED GIVE YOU THE
STRENGTH TO WALK THROUGH
LIFE FACING EACH NEW
SITUATION WITH COURAGE
AND OPTIMISM.

—ANONYMOUS

Chapter One

# OUCH! WHY TALK ABOUT IT?

*Why? Why must it be like this for so many of us? Why do so many people wish to see me fail? Why does everybody hate me? For some of us teens these questions go through our heads. I still can't figure out why I keep going. I am not afraid of death. I'm not afraid because I have cheated death too many times, and pain, I don't fear pain. Cuz nothing can hurt me worse than this! I still can't think of a reason or explanation for why I'm going through this. I've lost everything.... My job, my girl, my house, my friends, and my family. I would trade anything in the world, just to have it all back. This is where it ends. But before it's done, I have one more question "Can you feel my pain?"*

"Can you feel my pain?" Who hasn't asked that question or wanted to know the answer? If you've had painful experiences, you may feel that you're all alone. No one wants to feel that way. And the truth is, you're not alone. Everybody hurts because we're living in a broken, fallen world, and things are not the way they were created to be. This book will focus on the kinds of pain that come from abuse and abandonment.

Facing your pain is no small task. Many of your friends or family members may never pick up a book like this. You have, and that's a really big deal. By choosing to face your past, you can find freedom from it. It isn't easy—otherwise everyone would find healing, and abuse wouldn't be such a huge problem. You get to be different. You're doing this, and you'll make it through to the other side. Awesome! That's our motivation. Your long-term freedom and healing will be worth any pain you must experience along the way.

## Good Pain vs. Bad Pain

When we talk about facing pain, it's important to know there are two kinds of pain—good pain and bad pain. We experience good (healthy) pain when we experience something difficult or uncomfortable that forces us to grow. For example, if your girlfriend confronts you because she feels hurt that you don't return her phone calls, that's going to sting a little, right? It doesn't feel good when someone confronts you like that. Or, if you blow off a paper for English class, get an F, and as a result are grounded for the weekend. That feels bad, too. Both of those examples are of situations that are uncomfortable to walk through. They hurt. But when you move through them, you'll grow in your relationships and become more mature. You'll learn that your friends don't feel valued if you don't call them back. You'll learn that you can't blow off a responsibility at work or at school and that sometimes you must put work ahead of having fun. You can't—and shouldn't—try to escape those experiences of pain. That kind of pain has a purpose.

Bad pain is different—it goes beyond making you uncomfortable for the purpose of your growth. It causes damage to your heart and in your life. It disrupts God's design for you. So, if the same person who feels hurt that you never return phone calls spreads rumors about you online to ruin your reputation, and then you lose all of your friends, that's *bad* pain—that person's behavior is abusive. If you tell your parents you got an F on your English paper, and they respond by telling you that you're worthless, stupid, and will never accomplish anything in your life, then that's *bad* pain.

Those types of pain cause damage. In and of themselves, these experiences don't help us to mature. Instead, they can cause us to doubt our worth and our value, and they often hinder our growth.

I (Kristi) joined a gym earlier this year. I decided that I wanted to get in better shape and was feeling very excited and motivated at first. But now, I'm beginning to lose that motivation. It was fun at first, but the newness wore off. In fact, it's been more than a month since I've been to the gym. I know I should go back, but I'm really not excited about it. You know why? Because I know that when I go back, it'll hurt. I know my muscles will be sore after I start running and lifting weights again.

When I coached softball, the girls always said the same thing about the start of the season. During tryouts the girls would be so sore they couldn't move. But for any of us who have experienced that initial pain, we know it gets better, right? If we keep exercising, our muscles get stronger. Our bodies respond because they're made to exercise. The pain actually begins to feel kind of good. In fact, when I exercise regularly, I feel better. I have more energy, my attitude improves, and I actually look forward to the next time I get to work out.

Facing the pain of your past and feeling your emotions is kind of like that. At first, you may not want to do it. It hurts to go back to memories and emotions you haven't visited in a while. But, just like going to the gym, once you allow yourself to feel, you'll get stronger. Just like your muscles, your emotions will respond—they're made to be felt and expressed. We promise you, if you read through this book, complete the exercises, and share with someone what you're learning, you'll begin to grow. Yes, there will be some pain involved, but just like my trainer told me, "No pain, no gain!" The gain you'll experience from feeling and expressing your pain is healing and true freedom.

## Pain in the Bible

The Bible has a lot to say about your pain and your past and how to deal with them fully to find healing. Many people assume that facing your pain means feeling sorry for yourself. Those people would think that counseling and talking about the past; comes from a desire to have a pity party. "The past is the past, you can't change it—just move on." Or "Stop thinking about it—what's done is done." Or "The Bible says that you should 'forget what is behind,' so what's the point of looking at the past?"

It's common to hear Philippians 3:13 quoted as a reason not to look at the ugly parts of our lives (the things we've done and the things that have been done to us). Sometimes that seems easier and is tempting. It's true that in this verse the writer says, "But one thing I do: Forgetting what is behind and straining toward what is ahead." But when we read any Scripture, we must look at the big picture of what's being said. Have you ever had someone repeat something you said and totally mess it up by taking one part of the conversation out of context? The same is true here. So let's look at the big picture before we draw our conclusion.

You might be surprised to know that the man who wrote this book (and twelve other books in the New Testament), the apostle Paul, was originally a horrible, cruel abuser. He was a man who had grown up in a strict faith community. In fact, his commitment to what he thought the Hebrew Scriptures taught led him to physically abuse Christians. He had a history of torturing and killing Christians. He thought they were committing blasphemy by saying Jesus was God, and he was convinced that they needed to be forced into silence. He even felt proud for defending God in this way and believed his actions were earning God's approval.

> "I WENT AFTER ANYONE CONNECTED WITH THIS 'WAY,' WENT AT THEM HAMMER AND TONGS, READY TO KILL FOR GOD. I ROUNDED UP MEN AND WOMEN RIGHT AND LEFT AND HAD THEM THROWN IN PRISON. YOU CAN ASK THE CHIEF PRIEST OR ANYONE IN THE HIGH COUNCIL TO VERIFY THIS; THEY ALL KNEW ME WELL." (ACTS 22:4 *THE MESSAGE*)

Later, Paul became a Christian and had to deal with the reality that he had gravely hurt the very group of people whom he now held dear. Paul realized that the things he once did to try to earn God's approval actually displeased God (Acts 9:1–5). This helps us understand Paul's statement to forget the past and look to the future. Paul only said this immediately *after* talking honestly about his own painful past (Philippians 3:4–9). He had admitted, processed, and turned from his wrong beliefs that caused his abusive behavior. *That's* what allowed him to move ahead "toward the goal." We have to learn from the past before we can let go of it.

Pretending your pain doesn't exist doesn't help you—instead, it actually keeps you from moving forward. Your past could be filled with painful, hurtful actions toward others. Or you could look at your past and think you're perfect because you haven't done anything *that* bad. Either way, the truth is if you don't deal with your past, your past becomes your present, and it'll control you in the future. We're going to take some time to look at the reasons to do all of this emotional hard work.

## Reasons to Face Your Pain

> TO THE JEWS WHO HAD BELIEVED HIM, JESUS SAID, "IF YOU HOLD TO MY TEACHING, YOU ARE REALLY MY DISCIPLES. THEN YOU WILL KNOW THE TRUTH, AND THE TRUTH WILL SET YOU FREE." (JOHN 8:31–32)

### A WAY TO LIVE IN TRUTH

You may have grown up experiencing pain in your family but convinced yourself that your parents are perfect, they love you, and that *you're* the one who caused the problems—you blame yourself. You may have endured physical or sexual abuse by those who were supposed to love you. This distorts your view of what it means to be loved. This is why abused children, when they grow up, often begin dating abusive people. If a person connects feeling loved with pain, then that person will accidentally be attracted to new people who'll hurt him or her in similar ways.

Facing your pain allows you to call what has happened to you by its correct name: abuse, abandonment, molestation, etc. Then, you can begin to relearn the truth and what it means to have healthy relationships. We'll be helping you do that in the chapters ahead. For now, let's look at Lauren as an example:

Lauren was a sixteen-year-old who was involved in her church's student leadership group. She had the opportunity to attend a weekend retreat. This time away from home allowed the students to share, bond, and address their struggles. The last night of the retreat, the youth pastor held a time of sharing in which students were asked to tell what they learned from the experience. Toward the end of the share time, Lauren decided she had something to say. She cried as she said, "All my life I've heard people say, 'I love you.' My parents tell me, 'I love you,' but they never spend any time with me, and I hear them screaming at each other every night. My ex-boyfriend said he loved me, but he pressured me into having sex with him. And you know what? I don't think that's love anymore! This week I felt what real love is supposed to feel like, and I truly thank you for showing me that."

## LOVE IS PATIENT, LOVE IS KIND. (1 CORINTHIANS 13:4)

Lauren faced her brokenness and pain and, as a result, was able to destroy her distorted view of love and replace it with the truth of what love really is.

## A WAY TO EXPERIENCE HEALTHY RELATIONSHIPS

Facing the truth and the pain of your past is necessary to experience appropriate, healthy relationships in the present. If you act like the abuse that was done to you growing up was no big deal, then later, you're likely to minimize the abuse a boyfriend or girlfriend (or husband or wife) will do to you. Sadly, we often see this dynamic in action when students tell us that their moms keep going from one abusive man to another. We see it when students experience a series of relationships with unhealthy boyfriends or girlfriends who chronically mistreat them. If you have experienced these things, we know that it's a big deal and that you hurt. Even if no one else will acknowledge how hurtful this abuse is, we're telling you how wrong it is.

The biggest struggle I've ever had was when I had to live without a father. My real father left my mom to get drunk and party while she was pregnant.

I decided I would never trust a man again. Later, my mom met a man who would become my stepdad. I'd decided not to get too attached because I didn't think it would last. Eventually, he asked my mom to marry him, and of course she said yes. When they got married, I decided to try and get along with him and get to know him. It turned out that he was great and treated me like a daughter. I finally had all the love I'd never gotten from my father. He took me to games and told me the rules. My stepdad was the one who got me into sports. He played ball with me; and when I needed someone to talk to, he was there. He understood me. That's when I decided to accept him and not judge him, because not all guys are the same. My dad is my stepdad and no one else. My mom and stepdad have been married for six years, and I just found out that he is now going to adopt me! That means I'm going to have his last name, just like he's my real dad.

– Krista, age thirteen

By facing her past and the pain about her biological father, Krista was finally able to trust someone else to love her and give her the attention and time that she needed. What a great example of how new relationships can repair the old ones that have hurt us.

## A WAY TO BREAK DESTRUCTIVE FAMILY PATTERNS

If you've experienced abuse from your parents, then you don't want to repeat those patterns, right? Well, here's your chance to change. The sad reality is if you don't face your past, someday you'll be unable to meet your children's emotional needs and you could hurt them the same ways your parents did you. Unless you're whole and healthy, you'll be unable to meet another person's needs.

## Branden's Story

I (Kristi) met Branden when he was fifteen years old. Both he and his girl-friend were sophomores in high school, and she had just given birth to their son, Edgar. I spent quite a bit of time with Branden and his girlfriend talking about how to stay in school, make money, and be good parents to their baby.

Over and over Branden expressed his heartfelt desire to be a better dad than he'd had growing up. He explained that his father was rarely around; but when he was, Branden's dad would yell at Branden, cuss at him, and sometimes hit him. Branden also had vivid memories of his father abusing Branden's mother.

Generally, Branden felt that he was never good enough for his father and desperately wanted his approval, yet he also hated him for causing his family such pain. After Branden got his girlfriend pregnant at the end of ninth grade, Branden's relationship with his father was more strained than ever. The following illustrates one memory Branden has from his childhood:

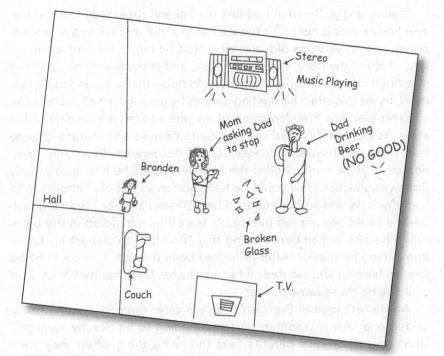

The music would be playing loud just to hide the fighting sounds, but I'd still wake up and see bad things. This scene was the worst for me. My dad had poured beer on my mom for no reason and also hit her in the face and made her bleed. He said it was an accident because he was drunk, but that's no excuse for what he did. My struggle is to be nothing like my father. I hate him with a great passion. I hate that I am a spitting image of him. I never wanna be like him! I try my hardest not to, but I hear people say, "Like father, like son." I know I am nothing like him, so I won't be. But I still struggle, hoping I will not be a woman beater, still hoping I will never go to jail.

– Branden, age nineteen

Branden was determined not to make the same mistakes his father had made, and, in the early months of Edgar's life, Branden expressed how much he loved his son and enjoyed spending time with him. After a lot of hard work, he and his girlfriend beat the odds. They graduated from high school, obtained full-time jobs, and were living together with their son in their own apartment.

However, about six months after graduation, things took a turn for the worse. One morning Branden's girlfriend called me at my office, crying. She explained that she and Branden had been having a lot of conflict. She told how Branden would often become angry with her or Edgar and begin to yell and swear at them. She said that there had been times when Branden became so angry that he pushed her.

That morning, Branden had lost control and repeatedly pushed her, eventually causing her to hit the kitchen counter and fall to the ground. Edgar, now three years old, was so scared he ran to the bathroom, sat down behind the door, covered his ears, and cried. Branden's girlfriend described other times when Edgar would throw things around the apartment, trying to distract his fighting parents by getting himself into trouble.

Later that day, Branden came to my office to tell me his side of the story. As we talked I could see Branden's posture and attitude change from anger and frustration to sadness and desperation. Eventually, Branden cried as he remembered the heartfelt words he had spoken only three years earlier. How could he have gotten so out of control that he had physically and verbally abused his girlfriend and son? Branden realized he could see himself in Edgar's scared face huddled in the bathroom. He also remembered being that "bad kid" to distract his father from hitting his mother. After all he had been through, how could he be just like his own abusive dad? If he hated what his father had done, how could he do those same things?

Abuse isn't logical! Branden's story is very common. Haven't we all said at one time or another, "I'm never going to be like my parents"? Don't you think your parents said the same thing when they were younger? Sure, every generation makes a few improvements, but when abuse is involved, a few small improvements aren't enough. We have to allow God to heal the pain of abuse. Keep reading because we're going to teach you how to do that.

## DO NOT BE LIKE YOUR FATHERS AND BROTHERS, WHO WERE UNFAITHFUL TO THE LORD. (2 CHRONICLES 30:7 NIV 1984)

If you break these destructive family patterns, it gives potential for a better relationship with your family. This doesn't happen all the time. Sometimes the people in our lives reject the opportunity to grow because it's too hard. But if and when they do, we can sometimes improve or restore those relationships.

**Q:** "But this is my family! Why would I want to hurt them by bringing up the past?"

**A:** "Remember, there's good pain and bad pain. The pain you experienced from your family, if it was abuse, was damaging. That was bad. If you choose to bring up the past and admit to your family that what happened to you was painful, what they'll feel is the good kind of pain—it's pain that can produce growth in your family members and in your relationships. It's okay to be honest if your desire for honesty is to cause growth. It's not okay to be honest if your desire is to get back at them by hurting them like they hurt you. Check your motives first, but don't protect your family from the truth just because it will make them feel bad."

## Breaking Through Denial

In my office I (Kristi) have a little refrigerator. I keep it stocked with Diet Coke for me, bottles of water for students, and some food for my lunches. When I returned from spring break last year, I opened my office door to find a little surprise. Apparently on the last day of school before spring break, the cleaning folks were making their rounds. When vacuuming my office they unplugged the fridge and never plugged it back in. When I returned ten days later and opened it, I had quite an unpleasant surprise—a stench that could peel paint off the walls. So I closed it right back up again!

I had a few options. I could decide to let it be and pretend I didn't own a little refrigerator—start keeping my food and drinks in the staff breakroom. But what's the truth? The refrigerator is there, and it still stinks! Maybe I could clean the outside to make it look real shiny so no one would know anything was wrong with it. But what's the truth? It still stinks! Or perhaps I could open it up (just for a second), spray some air freshener in there, and then close it again real fast. But what's the truth? It still stinks (probably a bit worse)!

What was the obvious answer to this problem of mine? Clean out the refrigerator! I avoided it all day, but eventually I had to do it. I cleaned out all of the moldy, stinky food from inside. My eyes watered, I had to squint my eyes, and I had to leave the door open for a while to air out my office. In the end it was worth it because the result was that my little refrigerator could be used just as it was designed—to keep my food and drinks cold.

We tend to come up with a lot of different ways to avoid facing the truth about the pain (or stink) in our lives, don't we? First we may try to *act* as if it's not even there. But what's the truth? Sometimes we make ourselves look good on the *outside* so everyone will *think* we're fine. But what's the truth? Other times we go for the quick fix and use drugs or alcohol to try and cover up the pain. But what's the truth? I think you get the idea.

Breaking through denial means admitting that there's something stinky going on in your life and deciding to do the hard work of getting it out. What we have to remember is the solution wasn't to throw away the refrigerator. The problem was the *food* rotting inside. In the same way, the solution is not to throw *you* away and accept Satan's lie that you are worthless and might as well not exist. But there *are* some attitudes, memories, and beliefs inside of you that need to get cleaned out. Once that happens, then, like my refrigerator, you'll be able to function as you were designed—to have loving, authentic relationships and to experience joy, freedom, and excitement with nothing holding you back!

## A WAY TO EXPRESS FAITH

The final reason to face your pain is that it's a powerful way to express faith in God. We realize that as you're reading this book, you might not be sure what you believe about God. Again, we know that when you experience deep pain and abuse that the very first thing to get messed up is your view of God. It's okay to keep reading if you're struggling with your faith. In fact, we think you'll find it helpful. By being willing to look at your pain and your past honestly, you're saying that you're willing to take the step of faith and give God a chance.

The Bible says that, "The LORD is close to the brokenhearted and saves those who are crushed in spirit" (Psalm 34:18). And in Matthew 5:4 Jesus pronounces a blessing on those who are willing to mourn (and keep on mourning). In fact, he goes on to say that those who face their pain are the ones who'll experience divine comfort from God himself. You'll experience these things, too. It's God's promise.

Maybe you need God to show you who he really is. He's not a God who passively sat by and allowed you to be hurt and abused. He's a God who came to earth to suffer and die for the human race. He is the One who'll return to triumph over all human evil (1 Corinthians 15:25–26; Revelation 20:7–15) and who is lovingly committed to bringing good out of your pain (Romans 8:28–39).

Even if your faith in God is small right now, facing your pain is a tremendous way to grow that faith and tell God you're willing to give him a chance to prove he is who he says he is.

# Chapter One Activities

## LEVEL ONE

What is keeping you from living the joyful, victorious life God intended? On the picture of the refrigerator on the following page, write the "stinky things" that you need to clean out of your life. These could be destructive memories, attitudes, habits, or feelings. In what ways do you—

*Ignore the problem* (act like there's nothing wrong)?
*Clean the outside* (make it look good to everyone else)?
*Spray air freshener* (come up with a quick fix to feel better)?

## LEVEL TWO

What makes facing your pain (a.k.a. cleaning out the refrigerator) difficult?

In this chapter, what encouragement stands out to you? Write that encouragement on a 3x5 card and use it as a bookmark as you work through the rest of this book. This can be your anchor when you feel like giving up.

We want you to know that it's not your job to heal yourself. God created you uniquely in his image, and right now he's creating a pathway of healing that's uniquely yours. That means you don't have to figure this all out for yourself. Pay attention to the memories, thoughts, and feelings that occur as you read these chapters. God is guiding this process and you can trust what he's bringing to mind. A very helpful tool to help you identify important memories and feelings connected with past pain is called the "mind-streaming activity." Set a timer for ten minutes and then, in a separate journal or in a notebook, write honestly about your painful feelings and memories. Write without editing or stopping until the timer goes off. This journaling is your private process. Later, you can share from it as you are comfortable.[1] Mind-streaming can help you connect to inner thoughts and feelings you are probably not fully aware of. As these toxic thoughts and feelings are brought out in the open through journaling, you can then take them to God, asking him to help you deal with them. All three of us practice this journaling process when we feel overwhelmed and stuck in our emotions.

## LEVEL THREE

Make an inventory of the people you have daily contact with. Include family members, friends, teachers, etc. Review this list and focus on the following two areas:

> Disrespectful or hurtful behaviors you are currently *experiencing* in your relationships…
> Disrespectful or hurtful behaviors you are *initiating* in your relationships…

In this chapter we looked at three reasons to face your pain: Facing your pain will (1) help you to live in truth, (2) build healthy relationships and break destructive family patterns, and (3) express your faith in God. Which of these reasons is the most appealing to you?

Chapter Two

# UNDERSTANDING ABUSE

I came to school and was supposed to tell everyone I fell down the stairs. That's what I said when my friends asked. I said it again when the teachers asked. I hope they believed me. The truth was the opposite, actually. I was dragged up the stairs. By my dad. He was mad 'cause I lied to him about my report card. I had to lie or he'd see I failed chemistry and he won't let me see Ezequiel. Prom is coming up and this is my last chance to go. We've been saving up and planning this for months, and I have to go! Anyway, when he found out, he got really mad and freaked out like he always does. It's not usually this bad though. He really let loose on me this time. It all happened so fast, I can't remember every detail. But I remember being dragged up the stairs 'cause I thought he was going to rip my hair out. Then I remember being thrown to the ground. Then there were punches to my face, and kicks to my legs, stomach, and arms. I remember lying on the ground in a ball, trying to get real small. Eventually it was over. The next day I wasn't allowed to go to school because of all the bruises. But grades are important in my family, so I had to go eventually. My mom caked makeup all over my face to cover the bruises and, even though it's hot out, I had to wear jeans and a long-sleeved shirt to cover the bruises on my arms and legs. And now, here I am…waiting to talk to the school counselor. Obviously, my friends and teachers didn't believe me, or I wouldn't be here. What should I do? If I tell the truth, things could get worse. If I lie, like they told me to, things could stay the same. I just want someone to help me. I just want it to stop. Maybe I can just hang on a few more years until I graduate and I can get out of here. But a few more years feels like an eternity. What should I do?

– Tineal, age sixteen

Obviously, abuse is painful. It's also confusing. You hate it and want it to stop, but you don't know if your choices will just make things worse. It may feel like you're left with impossible choices, none of which are clearly the right one. Sometimes you aren't even sure that what you've experienced is "abuse." You might think, *Don't most families have problems like this? Am I just being too sensitive?*

Thankfully, not everyone experiences the kind of physical violence Tineal suffered. But her abuse is much more common than we'd like to believe. And whether or not you've experienced the more extreme kinds of abuse, virtually all of us have experienced some form of pain and abandonment. Since there's no such thing as a perfect person, family, or community, all of us have been wounded by, and have wounded, others. As you read this book, you will no doubt see stories, quotations, or situations that you can relate to. We encourage you to read this book prayerfully and with an open mind and see what you can relate to and what might be affecting your life in a negative way.

No matter what kind of pain you've experienced, it's very real and also is unique to you. Don't compare yourself to anyone else. If something happened to you and it caused you pain, then it's important. In this chapter we're going to look at the pain of abuse, and the next chapter will deal with the pain of abandonment. If something applies directly to you, then we'd like to encourage you to underline it as you read. That will help you when you get to the activities at the end of each chapter.

## Types of Abuse That Wound

### PHYSICAL ABUSE

*Physical abuse* is defined as any injury (that's not an accident) to a child or teen by an adult or older caregiver. This could include hitting, slapping, kicking, shaking, burning, or any other physical assault that causes injury.[1]

**IN 2005-2006 ALMOST THREE MILLION AMERICAN CHILDREN WERE ABUSED OR NEGLECTED. MOST OF THE CHILDREN WHO WERE ABUSED SUFFERED PHYSICAL ABUSE.**[2]

Parents, including Christian parents, have different convictions about the types of discipline that are best and appropriate for their children. Some parents use spanking as a form of punishment and some don't. It's important for us to recognize that there's a critical difference between spanking and child abuse. State law is based on a simple principle: parental discipline shouldn't cause physical injury to the child. Biblical teaching harmonizes with this distinction because the purpose of biblical discipline is to build up a child to maturity. Physical discipline that injures a child tears down that child physically, emotionally, and spiritually. It's not okay to deliberately injure a child or teen.

Domestic violence can be broadly described as the use of physical violence (or the *threat* of physical violence) to control a family member.[3]

**IN AMERICA, MORE THAN 40 PERCENT OF ADULT FEMALE HOSPITAL EMERGENCY ROOM VISITS ARE CAUSED BY DOMESTIC VIOLENCE, AND ALMOST HALF OF THE WOMEN MURDERED IN THE UNITED STATES ARE MURDERED BY A HUSBAND, BOYFRIEND, OR EX.[4]**

The goal of domestic violence is to have power or influence over other family members, which causes them to "stay in line" out of fear. Domestic violence includes not only physical violence, but also *threats* of physical violence. Threats can include verbal threats, implied threats (harming pets, property, punching a wall, etc.), or threatening to harm family members.

**THEREFORE PRIDE IS THEIR NECKLACE;
THEY CLOTHE THEMSELVES WITH VIOLENCE.
FROM THEIR CALLOUS HEARTS COMES INIQUITY;
THE EVIL IMAGINATIONS HAVE NO LIMITS.
THEY SCOFF, AND SPEAK WITH MALICE;
WITH ARROGANCE THEY THREATEN OPPRESSION.
(PSALM 73:6-8)**

Some abusers will start by using physical violence against their partner or children, and then the violence will become less common because it has served its frightening, intimidating purpose. Once the abuser's physical violence has been experienced by family members, abusers can intimidate and control merely by making threats or by attacking family pets or possessions instead of by directly assaulting family members (which could land them in jail). Other abusers, however, continue to assault family members—some abuse their family members on a regular basis, and others are irregular and unpredictable. Whatever the pattern of physical abuse, it's always painful and very harmful.

## SEXUAL ABUSE

Sexual abuse occurs when someone uses (or exploits) a child or teen for his or her own sexual gratification through sexual contact or sexual interaction.

**AT LEAST ONE OUT OF THREE GIRLS AND ONE OUT OF SEVEN BOYS EXPERIENCE CHILDHOOD SEXUAL ABUSE.[5]**

**AMONG WOMEN THIRTY-ONE YEARS OLD AND YOUNGER, ALMOST 42 PERCENT REPORT HAVING EXPERIENCED AT LEAST ONE INCIDENCE OF SEXUAL ABUSE.[6]**

*Contact* sexual abuse is when physical contact is made. This can also be called *molestation*; and when it happens between family members, it's referred to as *incest*. Sexual contact happens in a variety of forms and severity, but *all* cause a great deal of damage.

Sexual abuse can occur even when there is no physical contact. That's called *interactive* sexual abuse. Interactive sexual abuse is the act of deliberately exposing a child or teen to sexual activity (images or information) that's not appropriate for his or her age.

Interactive sexual abuse occurs when a four-year-old is allowed to look at his dad's *Playboy* magazines, when a six-year-old watches sexually explicit movies with the babysitter, or when a thirteen-year-old has explicit sexual conversations with a young child on the school bus. When an older person puts his or her own sexual interests and pleasure ahead of the best interest of a child, that's abusive.

The picture below is called a continuum—it shows the range and types of sexual abuse. The least severe offenses are at the bottom, with increasingly severe forms of abuse as you ascend the chart.[7]

## SEXUAL ABUSE CONTINUUM

Most Severe

☐ Intercourse
☐ Attempted Intercourse
☐ Oral Sex
☐ Genital Contact
☐ Breast Contact
☐ Intentional Sexual Touching of Buttocks or Thighs
☐ Simulated Intercourse
☐ Touching of Clothed Breasts
☐ Sexualized Relationship
☐ Sexual Kissing
☐ Deliberate Exposure to Pornography or Sexual Activity
☐ Flashing/Exposing Body Parts
☐ Sexual Conversations with a Minor
☐ Sexual Nickname

Less Severe

Anytime the activities listed on the continuum occur and are unwanted, it's considered sexual abuse. That makes sense. But it's also abuse in certain cases when a child or teen *seems* to have willingly participated in the activity. We'll talk about characteristics of an abuser later, but it's important to know now that an abuser is quite skilled at tricking the victim into thinking they're willingly participating in the abuse (and even enjoying it). A child or teen *cannot* legally consent to sexual activity when there's a significant difference in power due to age and/or developmental status.

> BUT IF OUT IN THE COUNTRY A MAN HAPPENS TO MEET A YOUNG WOMAN ... AND RAPES HER, ONLY THE MAN WHO HAS DONE THIS SHALL DIE. DO NOTHING TO THE WOMAN; SHE HAS COMMITTED NO SIN DESERVING DEATH. THIS CASE IS LIKE THAT OF SOMEONE WHO ATTACKS AND MURDERS A NEIGHBOR.
> (DEUTERONOMY 22:25–26)

## EMOTIONAL ABUSE

*Emotional abuse* is a pattern of behavior that harms a child's emotional development and sense of self-worth.[8]

> THE TONGUE THAT BRINGS HEALING IS A TREE OF LIFE, BUT A DECEITFUL TONGUE CRUSHES THE SPIRIT.
> (PROVERBS 15:4 NIV 1984)

Emotional abuse includes excessive, aggressive, or unreasonable demands that place expectations on a child beyond his or her abilities. It includes using mind games (manipulation) to get the child to do what he or she is told.

Emotional abuse also occurs when an adult uses the child's emotions against him or her, or punishes a child for expressing emotions. All of our emotions are a very important part of who we are—even the painful ones. A child who gets yelled at or made fun of for crying or feeling scared or angry is experiencing a form of emotional abuse.

She comes home bottle in hand,
Her brain running loose as sand,
Sand running through my shaking fingers,
All I want is for her to stop the lingers,
I come to you hoping for snuggling,
You just go on juggling,
All I needed was an "I love you"

I used to stick to you like glue,
Oh how I was naive,
But you have lost me
and all you have left is to grieve.

– Ali, age thirteen

## VERBAL ABUSE

*Verbal abuse* is a form of emotional abuse in which words are used on purpose to put down, attack, blame, or cruelly control another person.[9] Many people who've endured physical or sexual abuse in addition to verbal abuse will report that years later the *verbal* attacks are what still haunt them the most. Verbal abuse cuts deep into our hearts and makes us doubt that we're important and that our feelings are accurate. Verbal abuse can stay with us long after any physical injuries have healed.

THE WORDS OF THE RECKLESS PIERCE LIKE SWORDS, BUT THE TONGUE OF THE WISE BRINGS HEALING. (PROVERBS 12:18)

My struggle is my mom. Sometimes I think to myself, "Does she really love me?" Sometimes I think, "My mom doesn't really even care for me." I can't talk to my mom. When I tell her something, she gets all mad at me and goes off. It's like anything I do, I do wrong. I will get yelled at for any little thing. When I try to do right, it's like she is telling me, "You can't do anything right." When I feel like this (which is like every day), it seems like I don't want to do anything the whole day. When I see my mom, I see her as just a lady that is just taking me in because she has to. She doesn't feel like my mom. I really don't know what a mom's love feels like. Yeah, she may say she loves me, but I really don't feel that she does.

– Jasmine, age fourteen

## SPIRITUAL ABUSE

*Spiritual abuse* is the inappropriate use of spiritual authority to force a person to do what's unhealthy.[10]

In high school I was very involved in my youth group at church. I had a lot of friends there, and I considered my youth pastor to be one of my best friends. I trusted him completely and wanted him to be proud of me. He taught me to depend on him to answer all my questions about God and to distrust myself. Sometimes I didn't agree with him and that would make him angry. He would use Bible verses to get his own way and to trick me into thinking I was wrong. I learned that if I was going to be accepted by him, I couldn't question what he told me.

Looking back, I can see that sometimes I was right and it was wrong of him to twist the Bible to get his own way. Even though I'm out of high school, I'm still scared of anyone in authority at a church. I'm afraid they're going to hurt me like my youth pastor did.

– Keeshauna, age twenty-two

When a pastor or other church leader uses his or her influence to control or manipulate a person, that's spiritual abuse. It could be manipulating someone into doing something that's actually illegal and morally wrong. It could also be convincing a person to do what's in the leader's best interest, using guilt to keep a person in line, or teaching that pleasing or obeying the leader is the only way to know God. Since spiritual leaders are seen as a representation of God, spiritual abuse distorts our view of God. So when a spiritual leader physically, sexually, or verbally abuses a person, it's also spiritual abuse.

[THE TEACHERS OF THE RELIGIOUS LAW AND THE PHARISEES] TIE UP HEAVY, CUMBERSOME LOADS AND PUT THEM ON OTHER PEOPLE'S SHOULDERS, BUT THEY THEMSELVES ARE NOT WILLING TO LIFT A FINGER TO MOVE THEM. (MATTHEW 23:4)

Another form of spiritual abuse is called *legalism*. Some people teach that the only way to earn God's love is by obeying a long list of rules and regulations.

When Jesus walked the earth, there were legalistic religious people who emphasized the importance of looking good on the outside and of gaining God's favor by keeping their long list of rules, in spite of the fact that their hearts were full of sin. These people were called Pharisees. Jesus repeatedly opposed them and angered them by his refusal to keep their rules. In fact, Jesus got very angry at the way *they* were leading people astray. In Matthew 23:25–26 Jesus says to them, "Woe to you, teachers of the law and Pharisees, you hypocrites! You clean the outside of the cup and dish, but [on the] inside [there is] greed and self-indulgence. Blind Pharisee! First clean the inside of the cup and dish, and then the outside also will be clean."

Jesus understood that when we focus on our inner heart being connected to the heart of Christ, eventually our outside actions and attitudes will automatically look more like Christ. Having a relationship with God isn't about trying to look good on the outside so others think everything is okay. It's also not about trying to earn God's approval by our actions. Having a vibrant relationship with God is about being honest with God and others about how we're struggling, and asking for help and support when we need it. God knows everything about us—including our weaknesses, our struggles, and our past that has shaped us. He graciously accepts us as we are and lovingly speaks truth into our lives so we can grow. Then, when we experience that kind of love and acceptance, our outside behavior will naturally change for the good.

## BULLYING

Abuse can occur in a variety of settings. We'll spend a lot of time talking about abuse in the context of our families because, sadly, that's where abuse is most prevalent. But abuse can also occur at school from the adults who should care for us, between friends, and between dating partners.

Bullying is something that occurs regularly and is often mistakenly blown off as a "part of growing up." "Boys will be boys," we hear people say. That's unfair and untrue. Bullying is a form of abuse, and it causes pain and damage. When one person uses power or status to make himself feel good at another's expense, that's abuse. The damage caused by this betrayal and rejection from our peers can cause wounds that are very deep.

We hear in the news about students who have committed suicide or homicide due to the bullying they experienced. Bullying is not a new concept, but today its forms and prevalence have greatly expanded due to the use of modern technology. Texting, instant messaging, email, blogs, social networking sites, and sexting provide abusers with anonymous ways to belittle and emotionally torture their victims in ways they might never have the nerve to do in person. In fact, part of the way that bullies feel powerful and dominant over their victims is by keeping their identity unknown. Being a victim of this type of abuse is particularly damaging because there's no "safe zone." Technology is everywhere, and going home from school is no longer a way to avoid a bully.

Online cyberbullying behaviors can then lead to other forms of abuse that occur in "real life." Once an abuser can get others on his side, his actions can escalate into more bold and brazen forms of abuse— destroying or defacing personal property, insulting and name-calling in person, or even physically attacking his victims. The same dynamics and effects of abuse apply if the perpetrator is a "friend."

If you have experienced, or are experiencing, this type of abuse from your peers, keep reading and apply the information we give you to your situation. Ask an adult for help. Talk about it. You're not alone. In fact, laws are changing to better address the issue of cyberbullying. Emails, texts, and information posted online can be retrieved (even after it was deleted by the user) by police and used to prosecute offenders. The myth of online anonymity is going away.

# Name Your Abuse

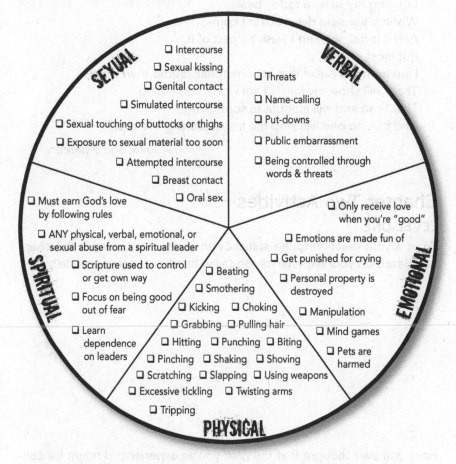

**SEXUAL**
- ☐ Intercourse
- ☐ Sexual kissing
- ☐ Genital contact
- ☐ Simulated intercourse
- ☐ Sexual touching of buttocks or thighs
- ☐ Exposure to sexual material too soon
- ☐ Attempted intercourse
- ☐ Breast contact
- ☐ Oral sex

**VERBAL**
- ☐ Threats
- ☐ Name-calling
- ☐ Put-downs
- ☐ Public embarrassment
- ☐ Being controlled through words & threats

**SPIRITUAL**
- ☐ Must earn God's love by following rules
- ☐ ANY physical, verbal, emotional, or sexual abuse from a spiritual leader
- ☐ Scripture used to control or get own way
- ☐ Focus on being good out of fear
- ☐ Learn dependence on leaders

**EMOTIONAL**
- ☐ Only receive love when you're "good"
- ☐ Emotions are made fun of
- ☐ Get punished for crying
- ☐ Personal property is destroyed
- ☐ Manipulation
- ☐ Mind games
- ☐ Pets are harmed

**PHYSICAL**
- ☐ Beating
- ☐ Smothering
- ☐ Kicking
- ☐ Choking
- ☐ Grabbing
- ☐ Pulling hair
- ☐ Hitting
- ☐ Punching
- ☐ Biting
- ☐ Pinching
- ☐ Shaking
- ☐ Shoving
- ☐ Scratching
- ☐ Slapping
- ☐ Using weapons
- ☐ Excessive tickling
- ☐ Twisting arms
- ☐ Tripping

We'd like to end this chapter with a poem written by a student reflecting on his abusive childhood. It's only when we look at where we have been that we are able to see where we want to go and know what changes to make. This poem shows us that even when we've experienced tremendous pain, our hope and determination don't have to die!

### I am from

I am from a torn home
Filled with a teary-eyed sister,
An angry, yet broken mother,
And an absent father, so full of rage.
I am from after-school loneliness,
Watching the other kids play games through my window,
Hearing my parents argue down the hall,
Hoping and praying they'd stop.

I am from late-night trips to my grandmother's house
Offering my sister a teddy bear,
Wishing the next day wouldn't come,
And if it did, wishing I wasn't a part of it.
But most of all,
I am from the belief that actions speak louder than words,
That I will show my family I am worth something,
That I can and will amount to something,
And that no one will stop me from reaching the top.

— Juan, age eighteen

## Chapter Two Activities

### LEVEL ONE

What is your reaction to the statistics on abuse mentioned in this chapter? Based on your experience, do these numbers seem accurate?

Have you ever thought that the pain you've experienced might be considered abuse?

Does naming any of your painful experiences as "abuse" make you feel better or worse about your situation?

## LEVEL TWO

Which areas of abuse have you experienced?

Who are the people in your life who have acted abusively toward you?

Look at the feelings chart in the Appendix at the end of this book (page 183). Choose two or three words that describe how you felt growing up and turn each feeling word into a sentence. "I felt _____ when _____. This feeling was expressed in the following ways: _____."

## LEVEL THREE

Create a timeline of your life and write the ten most significant events in your life so far. Put the positive events above the line and the negative events beneath the line. After you're done put a star next to those events you feel willing to share with a safe person.

### MY TIMELINE

Birth                                                                    Present

⟵——————————————————————————————————⟶

Chapter Three

# UNDERSTANDING ABANDONMENT

> My struggle was being without my mom. I had to take care of myself. I had to cook, clean, everything. Eventually I would run out of food, so I would depend on stealing it to live. And also, being alone so much, I didn't have anyone to tell me no or teach me right from wrong. No one gave me "the talk." I learned everything on my own. At a very young age, I got into drugs, which gave me money and stopped me from stealing food. But it also got me in deeper trouble and I couldn't get out. I begged my mom to come back and be my mom.
>
> – Amanda, age twenty

*Abandonment* (often called *neglect*) is when a parent or guardian fails to provide a child with the basic needs of life. This includes not only physical needs, but also emotional. Basically, if abuse is one side of the coin, then abandonment is the flip side. Physical, verbal, and sexual abuse involve acting in an inappropriate way, whereas abandonment involves someone failing to act.

Abandonment can be the most difficult form of pain to recognize and heal because it doesn't leave physical marks. Children often convince themselves that they never needed anything in the first place and that their home was fine. Later in this chapter you'll see an abandonment wheel that gives examples of all five types of abandonment. For now we'll take a closer look at the two most common types: physical and emotional.

## Types of Abandonment That Wound

### PHYSICAL ABANDONMENT
*Physical abandonment* is the failure of a parent or guardian to provide a minor with adequate food, clothing, medical care, protection, and supervision.[1]

**NEGLECT IS THE MOST COMMON FORM OF CHILD MALTREATMENT IN AMERICA. THE LARGEST AND MOST RECENT FEDERALLY FUNDED STUDY OF CHILD ABUSE AND NEGLECT FOUND THAT 77 PERCENT OF ABUSED CHILDREN WERE VICTIMS OF NEGLECT.**[2]

Physical abandonment is the most common reason that Child Protective Services becomes involved with a family. Some forms of physical abandonment seem obvious, such as depriving a child of the basic necessities of life such as food, water, or shelter. Not having those things can clearly endanger a child's life. But, just like other forms of abuse, abandonment has a wide range of how it is experienced (from most severe to less severe). Just because you had food, clothes, and a place to live doesn't mean you didn't experience some forms of abandonment. Some forms of physical abandonment are subtler and can be overlooked easily. (Remember, we're talking about our basic needs, not all of the things we want—such as a new iPod or $200 tennis shoes.) Here are some examples of situations that might help you to know if you have experienced this form of abandonment:

- You don't have enough food at home (you're chronically hungry).
- You don't have nutritious enough food for good health and energy (for example: hot Cheetos for breakfast).
- You don't have a jacket to wear when it's cold or shoes that fit.
- You don't receive regular medical care when you need it.

We want you to be aware that if your family didn't give you what you needed, for whatever reason, that can hurt and cause harm. Even if your family meant well and did the best they could, not getting what you need still causes damage—it's important to acknowledge that.

**IF ANYONE DOES NOT PROVIDE FOR HIS RELATIVES, AND ESPECIALLY FOR HIS IMMEDIATE FAMILY, HE HAS DENIED THE FAITH AND IS WORSE THAN AN UNBELIEVER. (1 TIMOTHY 5:8 NIV 1984)**

Another form of physical abandonment can be inadequate supervision. In an ideal world a child would always be supervised by her parent or guardian, but since many families require two incomes to pay the bills, it's often necessary that others help care for the children.

When parents work long hours but make *appropriate* arrangements for their children's care, that's *not* considered abandonment. "Adequate supervision" means that the majority of the time a capable adult is responsible for watching children in the home by providing meals, setting rules, and providing guidance and support. This adult could be the child's grandparent, aunt, uncle, or adult babysitter. It's also okay for a teenager to watch younger children for a few hours after school or for special occasions. However, it's not okay if a teen is required to drop out of school to care for her siblings. If a parent is at home, yet isn't paying attention because of a chronic illness or addiction, then they *still* aren't providing adequate supervision. That's also not okay. The bottom line is that when the consistent supervision (not just occasional babysitting) of young children is left to older children or teenagers, that can be a problem and a form of abandonment.

## WE WERE GENTLE AMONG YOU, LIKE A MOTHER CARING FOR HER LITTLE CHILDREN. (1 THESSALONIANS 2:7)

As a teenager, you look physically grown up, so sometimes parents and adults feel that they can leave you to take care of yourself and other siblings. But parenting young children is clearly a full-time job. Young children can't feed themselves, get themselves ready for school, or keep themselves safe. Just because teens need less physical help and direction doesn't mean their need for a parent goes away. Teenagers and young adults still need emotional support from their parents. You need someone to talk to when you've had a bad day. You need help navigating all the drama and difficult experiences that come with being in junior high, high school, and college. You're making huge life decisions, and when you're inadequately supervised, you don't have appropriate guidance. That leads us to our next form of abandonment: emotional.

## FOR YOU KNOW THAT WE DEALT WITH EACH OF YOU AS A FATHER DEALS WITH HIS OWN CHILDREN, ENCOURAGING, COMFORTING AND URGING YOU TO LIVE LIVES WORTHY OF GOD... (1 THESSALONIANS 2:11-12)

## EMOTIONAL ABANDONMENT

*Emotional abandonment* is the failure of a parent or guardian to provide a child or teen with adequate emotional support.

Everyone has always said, "Your dad is awesome"; "I love your dad"; "I wish I had your dad." But why didn't I see that dad? I just didn't understand. My dad gave me everything. I couldn't ask for more. I got everything I ever wanted. He even gave me a car. But I don't want material things. I want love, time, and understanding. All I can do is wait for my dad to realize the pain he has made me feel. As a kid when I heard the word "dad," I would think of support, endless love, and hugs. Now I think of pain, fear, and jealousy. Why didn't I see what others saw in you? Why didn't you use the words you say to others to me? That would make me happy. Then maybe I would have tears of joy and not pain.

– Christina, age sixteen

Many families can keep the other forms of abuse from happening, yet they still completely neglect the emotional needs of children. A child who doesn't have emotional support can develop very severe behavior problems or destructive ways to numb the pain.

Here's an example of how painful emotional abandonment can be: For years, counselors have known that many teens and young adults who cut themselves do so because they have a history of sexual abuse. That makes sense because sexual abuse is a very big deal and it causes great internal harm. We think it's interesting that after sexual abuse, another major factor associated with self-mutilation is coming from an emotionally neglectful home environment.[3] Another term that's commonly used is an "invalidating home environment," which means a home where it's not okay to feel and express emotions.[4] Wow! Not meeting a child's emotional needs causes some *very* profound damage—in fact, some of the *same* harmful effects caused by sexual abuse. Emotional abandonment is a very big deal.

There are major consequences to being deprived of physical touch and human relationship. It is likely that a person deprived of these things would be depressed, develop eating disorders or drug or alcohol problems, start cutting herself, and even become suicidal when emotionally neglected.

The reason that emotional abandonment (and all other forms of abandonment and abuse) affects us in such a profound way is that we're made for relationships that are nurturing and protecting. We, as humans, are made in the image of God and created for intimacy. No, we're not talking about sex. That's only *part of* intimacy. *Intimacy* is defined as "knowing and being known." That just means that deep down we desire to truly know others (mentally, emotionally, and spiritually) and to be known by others in return. It's not just something that we'd *like* to have or *prefer* to have. It is a *need* in our soul. So when we're abused or abandoned, in a way it tears the relational part of our soul.

## Connected yet Disconnected

I (Celestia) worked with a teenage girl I'll call "Julie." She and her parents came to see me because she was struggling with depression and an eating disorder. Julie came from a family that looked good on the outside. Her parents were married, had a nice home, and went to church regularly. Julie's friends may have thought her life was very good. In fact when they visited her house, they envied how much cool stuff she had. She had her own TV in her room, her own laptop, iPod, and cell phone. Her brother had all the best gaming systems in his room. Both parents had their own home offices with updated computer systems and flat screen TVs. When Julie came to see me, she couldn't understand why she was struggling with her weight and why she was feeling so sad. She even admitted that she felt guilty for feeling so bad because she knew that she had it "so good" compared to so many others.

As we talked we discovered that Julie felt completely alone in her family. Every day when Julie and her brother came home from school, they found their own dinner and spent the rest of the evening in their bedrooms. She would get online, watch TV, and text friends from school. She felt alone. She was alone. She had the company of all the glowing screens around her, but they didn't meet the need for relationship within her heart. She longed for her parents or her brother to come out of their own cyber worlds and pursue her—her heart, her hopes, her dreams. She was experiencing abandonment.

We know many students like Julie. In fact, you may be able to relate to this family. It's common for families to be busy with outside distractions and then come home and fill the remaining gaps with technology. It's easy to ignore the people in front of us and give priority to "virtual relationships" found on the computer or television. Julie was only able to step out of her loneliness as she became willing to put down the false relationships of texting and Facebook and replace that time with actual people who could talk with her, look her in the eye, and offer her comfort and support in the moment.

Technology is great and has given us more freedom and resources than we've ever had before. However, it also has no boundaries or respect for what we need. It demands we respond every time we hear a beep, and we, like slaves, immediately obey.

We want you to consider the amount of "screen time" you have in a given day. Compare that to the amount of "face-to-face time" in that same day. In order to be healthy and emotionally fulfilled, your amount of face time needs to be greater than your screen time.

| Examples of Screen Time | Examples of Face Time |
| --- | --- |
| Texting | Being with other people |
| Instant Messaging | Talking to the person you're with |
| Emailing | Being focused on one thing at a time |
| Talking on the phone | Making eye contact |

| Screen Time (cont.) | Face Time (cont.) |
|---|---|
| Watching TV or movies | Responding to what a person says |
| Playing video games | Asking questions |
| Playing online games | Being interested (and showing it) |
| Spending time on Myspace/ Facebook | Expressing empathy (feeling what others feel) |
| Surfing the Web | Offering or receiving encouragement |
| Listening to an iPod | Demonstrating affection (hugs, high-fives, pats on the back) |

None of us are going to throw our cell phones, TVs, or computers in the trash. We all appreciate the convenience and pleasure these forms of technology bring to our lives. But we're suggesting that we become aware that technology can rob us of what our hearts long for. We encourage you to set some boundaries for yourself so that you can stay connected—connected in real time, to real people, for relationships that last and satisfy.

## TAKE THE CHALLENGE: BE WHERE YOUR FEET ARE

I (Kristi) have a friend who gets frustrated with me whenever I'm hanging out with her and texting someone else. She tells me to put my phone away and "be where my feet are." She means that I need to be "present" with her and just be with her. When I'm texting, my mind is not with her in that moment. I realize that she's right. I'm trying to have two conversations at once, and that's really pretty disrespectful to the person who is making actual time to spend with me in real life. So this challenge is also for me as I try to practice this principle in my own life.

For a whole day, let's try to be where our feet are. If you're at lunch with your friends, put down your phones and talk to each other. When you're in class, be in class and listen to what's going on. After school, if you're walking home with friends, be with them and have a conversation with them as you go. When you're having dinner with your family, turn off all the screens around you (phones, iPods, TVs, etc.) for thirty minutes and talk to each other about what's going on in your lives. (Your parents are gonna freak!) Basically, this is a way to value and respect the people you're with. Plus, you're going to enjoy it a lot more, too.

### Pledge:

When given the opportunity, I will choose the most real form of communication possible. I will choose:

Face over phone...
...phone over email...
...email over text/IM.

# Acknowledge Your Abandonment

The following diagram visualizes some of the many ways we can experience abandonment.

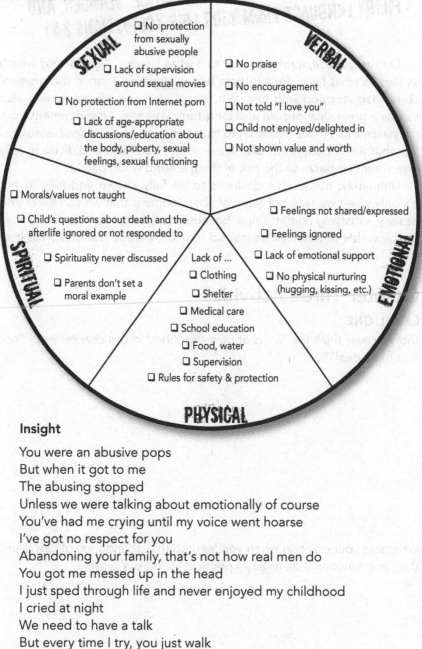

**SEXUAL**
- No protection from sexually abusive people
- Lack of supervision around sexual movies
- No protection from Internet porn
- Lack of age-appropriate discussions/education about the body, puberty, sexual feelings, sexual functioning

**VERBAL**
- No praise
- No encouragement
- Not told "I love you"
- Child not enjoyed/delighted in
- Not shown value and worth

**SPIRITUAL**
- Morals/values not taught
- Child's questions about death and the afterlife ignored or not responded to
- Spirituality never discussed
- Parents don't set a moral example

**PHYSICAL**
Lack of ...
- Clothing
- Shelter
- Medical care
- School education
- Food, water
- Supervision
- Rules for safety & protection

**EMOTIONAL**
- Feelings not shared/expressed
- Feelings ignored
- Lack of emotional support
- No physical nurturing (hugging, kissing, etc.)

## Insight

You were an abusive pops
But when it got to me
The abusing stopped
Unless we were talking about emotionally of course
You've had me crying until my voice went hoarse
I've got no respect for you
Abandoning your family, that's not how real men do
You got me messed up in the head
I just sped through life and never enjoyed my childhood
I cried at night
We need to have a talk
But every time I try, you just walk
Like how you walked out of my life
I was just trying to give you insight

– Cody, age sixteen

**BUT NOW YOU MUST ALSO RID YOURSELVES OF ALL SUCH THINGS AS THESE: ANGER, RAGE, MALICE, SLANDER, AND FILTHY LANGUAGE FROM YOUR LIPS. (COLOSSIANS 3:8)**

On the outside, it might seem as if what "Cody" experienced wasn't as bad as what his older brothers had experienced, since the physical abuse had stopped with him. But, as you can see, abandonment also causes a great deal of pain and long-term damage. Abandonment from our parents can make it difficult to trust in future relationships because of fear that those people will also leave. It can also make it difficult to fully love someone because the risk of them leaving is too painful.

Ultimately, our heart's desire is to be fully known and fully loved. It's only when we face our fears of abandonment that we can enter into healthy, satisfying relationships. Because the pain of abandonment may not be visible to others, it's essential to acknowledge it and express it so it can be healed.

## Chapter Three Activities

### LEVEL ONE

Did you ever think the forms of pain described in this chapter were "not that big a deal"?

What was your reaction when you learned that abandonment can cause the same emotional damage as physical and sexual abuse?

Can you relate to the idea of "technological abandonment"? Do you ever feel lonely even though you're "connected" constantly to others via your phone or computer?

## LEVEL TWO
Which areas of abandonment have you experienced (physical, emotional, verbal, sexual, spiritual)?

How does that abandonment impact you today in your relationships?

What steps are you willing to take this week to choose less "screen time" and get some "face time" back into your life? How can you encourage your friends and/or family members to do the same?

**LEVEL THREE**

On a separate piece of paper, complete the following sentence as many times as you need to:[5]

"I experienced _____ abandonment by (name the person)."

Do ten minutes of mind-streaming journaling (see the exercises at the end of chapter one that explain this tool). Focus on memories, thoughts, and feelings surrounding the abandonment you identified in the previous question.

# PART TWO

# When Your Relationships Hurt

BEING UNWANTED, UNLOVED, UNCARED FOR, FORGOTTEN BY EVERYBODY, I THINK THAT IS A MUCH GREATER HUNGER, A MUCH GREATER POVERTY THAN THE PERSON WHO HAS NOTHING TO EAT.

—MOTHER TERESA

Chapter Four

# IMPERFECT FAMILIES—
# IMPERFECT PEOPLE

A *dysfunctional family* is any family that doesn't function in a healthy way. At some level *every* family is dysfunctional because all of us are sinful. We don't always treat each other the way God intended. Each person and family is imperfect. We hurt and fail each other even when we don't intend to. But some families are dysfunctional in more specific ways and hurt each other more deeply. For example, a dysfunctional family would include abusive families (on the far end of the spectrum), as well as a family where one or both parents is addicted to drugs or alcohol. When parents get divorced that's also a form of dysfunction because, ideally, we would all benefit from having our parents stay together and get along well. Broken families generally experience much pain and damage.

No matter what the circumstances look like on the outside, a dysfunctional family is a family in which problems are constant and children's needs are left unmet on a regular basis. Keep in mind that families that look good on the outside may, in fact, be unhealthy. There may not be bruises, police involvement, drugs, or divorce, but the family could still be unhealthy.

The most significant characteristic of unhealthy families is that there's very little honest, healthy communication. Problems are not discussed or resolved, and feelings and needs are not acknowledged or responded to. Expectations, rules, and consequences aren't made clear. In unhealthy families there are *unspoken* rules. Everyone intuitively knows that certain topics are never to be brought up or discussed, so no one ever does. Children are left to figure this out themselves—despite the fact that they don't have the resources to do so. It leaves kids feeling frustrated and alone.

**Family Portrait**

In our family portrait
We look pretty happy
Let's play pretend, let's act like it
Comes naturally[1]

– P!nk (2001)

I (Kristi) have never heard a song that shows the thoughts and feelings of a child living in an unhealthy family better than "Family Portrait" does. Many of the themes discussed so far can be seen in these lyrics—looking good on the outside (looking happy in the family portrait), fear of divorce, parents' actions being unpredictable, children feeling responsible for the parents' feelings and actions, and perfection being expected. All unhealthy families are hurtful and cause damage. External bruises are horrible, but those are only one indicator of the pain caused by unhealthy families.

## What Does a Healthy Family Look Like?

Sometimes it's hard to picture what a healthy family looks like. In healthy families, feelings are allowed to be felt and expressed. For example it's okay to feel hurt by something another person in your family has done—even if they didn't do it on purpose. When that happens in healthy families, it's okay to call that out and talk it through. When there's conflict, family members talk about it openly and work to find a resolution that makes everyone feel valued and respected.

The following checklist will show you the clear, noticeable differences between unhealthy and healthy families:[2]

# PUT A CHECK NEXT TO ANY CHARACTERISTIC THAT DESCRIBES YOUR FAMILY

## In UNHEALTHY families:

- ❏ There is drug/alcohol dependency.
- ❏ Parents' relationship feels insecure.
- ❏ Problems are constant and unresolved.
- ❏ Looking good to others is prioritized/demanded.
- ❏ Children's needs are consistently unmet.
- ❏ There is fear of abuse (any kind).
- ❏ Parents' actions are unpredictable.
- ❏ Children fend for themselves.
- ❏ Perfection is expected/demanded.
- ❏ Children take on parents' responsibilities.
- ❏ Painful emotions are not allowed.
- ❏ Kids are responsible for their parents' feelings.
- ❏ Rules and consequences are unpredictable.
- ❏ Parents are too strict or too permissive.
- ❏ The family must always look good to others.

## In HEALTHY families:

- ❏ There are no active addictive behaviors.
- ❏ Parents' relationship feels stable.
- ❏ Problems are temporary and are resolved.
- ❏ Being "real" with others is encouraged.
- ❏ Children's needs are consistently met.
- ❏ There is respect without the fear of abuse.
- ❏ Parents are predictable and dependable.
- ❏ Parents meet their children's needs.
- ❏ Mistakes are used to learn/grow.
- ❏ Age-appropriate expectations and responsibilities are given.
- ❏ Emotions are expressed and responded to.
- ❏ Everyone is a responsible for their own feelings.
- ❏ Rules/consequences are stated/predictable.
- ❏ There is a balance of rules and relationship.
- ❏ The family is the same in public as it is in private.

We want to show you a couple examples of healthy family characteristics. Robert and Jason are both twenty-year-old students who grew up in healthy families. That doesn't mean that things were perfect—they each experienced their fair share of problems and conflicts growing up. But each of them felt safe in his own home, never feared being hurt physically or emotionally, and was taught how to resolve conflicts and face problems head on. If you were to meet Robert or Jason, you'd like them. They're both regular guys—they enjoy sports, weightlifting, and other "guy" things, but they also know how to communicate and express themselves in a healthy way.

In my family we learned how to emotionally connect with one another, meaning, we learned to be open with our feelings, thoughts, and concerns. This takes a lot of work and it's painful at times, but it's always worth it because we're all very close. Growing up with two sisters, it would have been easy to think that it's normal for girls to share their feelings and emotions, but not for guys to do the same. In our culture guys are told that real strength is found in being "tough and nonemotional" and that revealing our feelings is a sign of weakness. However, I grew up in a home that allowed me to show my emotions and talk about them—like when I was sad, afraid, worried, or even angry (as long as I was respectful). My parents didn't ridicule me for that. They actually encouraged it. In fact, since my dad showed his emotions, too, I learned that it takes a real man to be honest with himself and those he loves about how he feels.

– Robert, age twenty

## FATHERS, DO NOT AGGRAVATE YOUR CHILDREN, OR THEY WILL BECOME DISCOURAGED. (COLOSSIANS 3:21 NLT)

## FATHERS, DO NOT PROVOKE YOUR CHILDREN TO ANGER BY THE WAY YOU TREAT THEM. RATHER, BRING THEM UP WITH THE DISCIPLINE AND INSTRUCTION THAT COMES FROM THE LORD. (EPHESIANS 6:4 NLT)

In my family there were always rules and stuff, but any time I got in trouble it ended up being a positive experience. My parents didn't just yell and jump to conclusions. They sat me down and explained why I was being punished and why it would be good for me. One example I can think of is in high school when I got in trouble for smoking weed. My friend's parents found out first, and they ended up calling my dad. My dad came to me and said, "Do you know what that phone call was about?" By the tone of his voice I could tell that he knew, so I just told him, "Yeah, me and Alex were smoking weed." (I knew there was no point in lying.) It's funny because that whole experience ended up bonding me and my dad. He stayed real calm and told me how he did the same thing when he was young and how stupid it is because everything I do hurts me and all the others around me. He said that if this is the worst thing I ever do that we'd be all right. My dad said no matter what I do, he loves me but that he was disappointed in me. I know my dad cares about me and he always helps.

me out. When my mom came home, I was worried she'd freak out but she didn't. She told me how some people in her family made the mistake of trying drugs and it ended up ruining their lives. I never felt afraid of my parents, but I did feel real disappointed that I had let them down, and I wanted to apologize for that. I just thought, "Wow, that was stupid! Why did I do that? Why did I break their trust?" Actually, I kind of felt relieved when they found out. I knew other people knew and it was going to come out eventually. They did end up grounding me for two months, and I couldn't do anything. But since I didn't challenge them and showed them I was going to listen, I ended up not being grounded for as long as they said. But it was still about a month.

– Jason, age twenty

When we read the examples of Robert and Jason, we might be tempted to think that they've come from a long line of perfect families. However, what's interesting is that both Robert's and Jason's parents came from their own backgrounds of painful upbringing. In fact, Jason's mom grew up experiencing deep pain from her unhealthy family. Her father has spent most of her life in prison; and while she was in high school, her mother was killed by a drunk driver. However, God brought her to a place of healing, and she and her husband have worked hard to reverse the pain and dysfunction that could have been brought into their family.

Healing damage from the past involves understanding how others have wounded us. Our families provide one of the settings where we can be hurt, but our pain can also come from individuals outside our families. It's important that we are able to identify who's a safe person and who's not. Had Jason's mom not known how to identify a safe guy, she likely would have married an unhealthy man and Jason's experience growing up would have looked very different.

## Understanding Abusive People

The amazing thing about abusive people is that they generally don't stand out. You've heard the phrase, "You can't judge a book by its cover"? The same is true for abusers. They're not just creepy guys in trench coats or big, mean women on welfare. There's not an accurate single picture of an abuser. Abusers can come from any race, gender, income level, or walk of life. Abusers can be teachers, lawyers, salesmen, police officers, artists, bus drivers, etc. Abusers are regular people and cannot be predicted by race, ethnicity, occupation, personality, education level, or facial features. Yet, all abusers do have four common characteristics.[3] We want you to know these characteristics so you can spot an abusive person—either in your family, dating relationships, or friendships.

## BLAMING OTHERS

The first characteristic of abusers is that they don't believe their behavior was wrong, and they convince themselves that the victim was at fault.

Abusers are typically unwilling to accept full responsibility for their behavior. Rarely do abusers admit that they did something wrong—even after they've been arrested, convicted, and jailed for their crimes. For instance, rapists may say their victims were asking for sex by the way they dressed. Parents who abuse their children may say that the child should know not to behave badly in the evening when the parents are tired after work, or a church leader who verbally abuses his wife may quote a Bible verse that he interprets to say that he owns his wife and can do as he pleases.

Even child molesters may claim that their young victims consented to having sex or even that the child initiated the sexual activity. This shows the extreme break from reality abusers reach in order to live with themselves.

[AHAB WAS ONE OF THE MOST WICKED AND ABUSIVE KINGS OF ISRAEL. GOD SENT A DROUGHT ON THE LAND BECAUSE OF HIS SIN. WHEN THE GODLY PROPHET ELIJAH CAME TO AHAB TO CONFRONT HIS BAD BEHAVIOR, AHAB SHIFTED THE BLAME AWAY FROM HIMSELF.] WHEN HE SAW ELIJAH, HE SAID TO HIM, "IS THAT YOU, *YOU TROUBLER* OF ISRAEL?"

[ELIJAH IMMEDIATELY GAVE HIM A REALITY CHECK.] "I HAVE NOT MADE TROUBLE FOR ISRAEL," ELIJAH REPLIED. "BUT YOU AND YOUR FATHER'S FAMILY HAVE. *YOU* HAVE ABANDONED THE LORD'S COMMANDS." (1 KINGS 18:17–18, EMPHASIS ADDED)

## TRICKING OTHERS

Abusers say and do things that allow them to abuse and then *cause the victim to believe* that the abuse was his or her fault.

In order for abusers to escape the pain associated with doing something wrong, they must figure out a way to ease their own guilty conscience. In order to do this, abusers make themselves look like the victim and the abused feel that they did something wrong. Abusers can be quite skilled at manipulating words and actions to confuse the people around them and put others on the defense. Here are some examples:

"Other people just don't understand me. That's just how I am; and if you loved me, you'd know how to make me happy."

"You always make me so angry."

"You're too sensitive. I was only kidding. Why do you take things so personally?"

"My daughter is such a troublemaker. She's making the whole thing up. You're not going to believe her over me, are you?"

"If you really loved me, you'd let me do what I want."

"Your parents don't understand you—they don't love you like I do. Let me show you what love is all about."

SO AMNON LAY DOWN AND PRETENDED TO BE SICK. AND WHEN [HIS FATHER, KING DAVID] CAME TO SEE HIM, AMNON ASKED HIM, "PLEASE LET MY SISTER TAMAR COME AND COOK MY FAVORITE DISH AS I WATCH. THEN I CAN EAT IT FROM HER OWN HANDS." SO [HIS DAD] AGREED AND SENT TAMAR [TO HIM].

THEN [AMNON] SAID TO TAMAR, "[B]RING THE FOOD INTO MY BEDROOM AND FEED IT TO ME HERE." SO TAMAR TOOK HIS FAVORITE DISH TO HIM. BUT AS SHE WAS FEEDING HIM, HE GRABBED HER AND DEMANDED, "COME TO BED WITH ME, MY DARLING SISTER."

"NO, MY BROTHER!" SHE CRIED.

BUT AMNON WOULDN'T LISTEN TO HER, AND SINCE HE WAS STRONGER THAN SHE WAS, HE RAPED HER. (2 SAMUEL 13:6-7, 10-12, 14 NLT)

## JUDGING OTHERS

Abusers are very critical of other people and frequently point out everyone else's mistakes. They behave this way in order to shift the focus onto others, rather than on themselves. They do this because they don't want anyone to call them out on their behavior. They don't even want to admit to *themselves* that they're doing anything wrong. Abusers *should be* ashamed of themselves for what they're doing. That shame should move them toward changing their behavior. But since that shame is painful and they don't want to deal with it themselves, they cast it onto others around them. The more that abusers can point out what other people are doing wrong, the easier it is for them to deny and hide their guilt.

Abusers use the mistakes of others (coming home late, fighting with siblings, forgetting a birthday, leaving dirty clothes on the floor, doing poorly in school, wasting allowance, spilling milk during dinner, etc.) to justify their own abusive actions. It's also important to note that the more friends or family members try to point out the abuser's behavior, the more aggressive he'll become at identifying and scrutinizing the mistakes or weaknesses of others. This makes it even harder for victims to stand up for themselves and get help, since speaking out seems to make things worse.

"DO NOT JUDGE, OR YOU TOO WILL BE JUDGED. FOR IN THE SAME WAY YOU JUDGE OTHERS, YOU WILL BE JUDGED, AND WITH THE MEASURE YOU USE, IT WILL BE MEASURED TO YOU.

"WHY DO YOU LOOK AT THE SPECK OF SAWDUST IN YOUR BROTHER'S EYE AND PAY NO ATTENTION TO THE PLANK IN YOUR OWN EYE? HOW CAN YOU SAY TO YOUR BROTHER, 'LET ME TAKE THE SPECK OUT OF YOUR EYE,' WHEN ALL THE TIME THERE IS A PLANK IN YOUR OWN EYE? YOU HYPOCRITE, FIRST TAKE THE PLANK OUT OF YOUR OWN EYE, AND THEN YOU WILL SEE CLEARLY TO REMOVE THE SPECK FROM YOUR BROTHER'S EYE." (MATHEW 7:1–5)

## INTIMIDATING OTHERS

Abusers will say and do anything to scare their victims into hiding the abusive behavior from others.

Abusers build their lives around doing everything they can in order to avoid feeling guilt or facing any consequences. They must keep their victims silent at all costs. If a victim tells the truth and involves other people (especially other adults), then the abuser could get in trouble and be forced to change his behavior. Scaring the victim helps keep the abuse secret and allows it to continue. Sometimes the abuser is bold and actually threatens to kill the victim, the victim's family, or a beloved pet if he or she tells anyone.

Other times, the intimidation is subtle and abusers give mean looks or use angry body language to convey their threats. Intimidation adds to feelings of shame and powerlessness because the victim feels he or she can't do anything to escape the painful situation.

[IN THE EIGHTH CENTURY B.C., THE PEOPLE OF GOD WHO LIVED IN JERUSALEM WERE FACING A NIGHTMARE THREAT. A VICIOUSLY ABUSIVE ASSYRIAN GENERAL SURROUNDED THE CITY WITH HIS ARMY AND DEMANDED THAT THEY UNCONDITIONALLY SURRENDER TO HIS FORCES. HE INTIMIDATED THEM BY SAYING IF THEY PUT UP A FIGHT, THEN THEY WOULD EXPERIENCE EVEN WORSE SUFFERING.]

[HE SPECIFICALLY THREATENED THE LEADERS BY SAYING,] "FOR WHEN WE PUT THIS CITY UNDER SIEGE, [THE PEOPLE] WILL SUFFER ALONG WITH YOU. THEY WILL BE SO HUNGRY AND THIRSTY THAT THEY WILL EAT THEIR OWN DUNG AND DRINK THEIR OWN URINE." (2 KINGS 18:27 NLT)

## Responding to the Truth

It's difficult looking at these characteristics of abusers. Maybe reading these descriptions has brought up some bad memories and uncomfortable feelings. We want to end with an example of how we can respond in a healthy way to the painful truth about abusers—especially when we haven't previously realized or admitted a person was abusive.

Heidi, the mother of one of my (Kristi's) students, came into my office because her family was falling apart. She explained that a week earlier, her husband had been unexpectedly arrested for molesting young girls in the neighborhood. She didn't know what to do. Her marriage and family were collapsing. Heidi described her husband to me: He was an upstanding member of the community, he held a full-time job, he loved spending time with their fourteen-year-old daughter and ten-year-old son, and they went on family vacations together. The list went on and on. Most people who heard that this "nice" man had been accused of sexually abusing young girls refused to believe it. Family, friends, and members of the family's church were outraged and stated that he wasn't capable of such horrible crimes.

It's very difficult to admit that an abuser could be the "guy next door" because it feels scary. We want to believe that abusers stand out and are easy to spot. This is a very common and dangerous mistake.

What impressed me most about Heidi was that she was one of the few people who did not buy this false belief that "you'll know an abuser when you see one." Heidi was willing to face the painful possibility that her husband could, in fact, be a child molester. She also faced the devastating possibility that her husband might have molested one of their own children.

Approximately six months later her worst fear came true when her ten-year-old son admitted to her that he'd been molested as well. Heidi's husband was convicted of several counts of child sexual abuse, is currently spending time in jail, and will forever be labeled a sex offender. Because of Heidi's willingness to reject this common myth, her young son felt safe enough to come forward and start the process of healing from his abuse.

## Chapter Four Activities

### LEVEL ONE

Look back at the checklist on page 57 and, if you haven't done so yet, check the boxes that describe your family. Did you check more healthy or unhealthy characteristics?

Take some time to journal about your family. How would you describe your family to someone on the outside? If one of your friends were going to join your family, what would he or she need to know in order to "make it"? What topics are never talked about? What rules around the house must never be broken?

## LEVEL TWO

Have you ever thought that you would "know an abuser when you saw one"? Why might it be dangerous to continue to believe this?

Have you ever been blamed, tricked, judged, or intimidated by someone in your life? Until now, had you ever considered that person's behavior to be abusive? When, in past relationships, have you blamed yourself for an abuser's hurtful actions?

## LEVEL THREE

Draw two pictures of your family—draw first how your family looks to people on the *outside,* and second, draw how your family really is on the *inside.* If you're not comfortable drawing, you could make a collage of your family using pictures or words from magazines.[4]

Write in your journal about how it feels to have "two families:" the one other people see and the one that exists behind closed doors. What do you feel after doing this exercise?

Chapter Five

# UNDERSTANDING FRIENDSHIP AND DATING

## A MAN OF *TOO MANY* FRIENDS *COMES* TO RUIN, BUT THERE IS A FRIEND WHO STICKS CLOSER THAN A BROTHER. (PROVERBS 18:24 NASB)

## Friendship

At every stage of life, our friendships are important. But as a teenager, your friendships are more important to you than at any other time. When you were a kid, you made friends based on shared interests: you were in the same class at school, you were on the same sports team, or maybe you both liked the same color. Friendships were pretty easy.

But now, as a teenager, you're more mature and sophisticated. Your brain has the ability to do something it's never done before: you now have the ability to think abstractly. That means you can wonder, dream, and imagine. You now go through the world realizing that the people around you have their own thoughts and opinions—and some of those thoughts or opinions could be about *you*.

As teenagers and adults, abstract thinking makes us begin to wonder what others think about us and if the way they act toward us matches what they really think or feel inside. We begin to judge ourselves by what others *may* think about us, and we desperately want affirmation from others that we're okay. We now look to *each other* to validate us. The problem is, the people we think can make us feel okay are also struggling with the same insecurities.

The other thing that changes in our relationships when we became teenagers is that we no longer develop friendships in the simple way we did when we were young. It becomes less about shared interests or activities and more about intimacy—talking about what's important to us: our hopes, fears, dreams, and frustrations. With these discussions come issues of trust, confidentiality, betrayal, and conflict. We learn (sometimes through disappointment and pain) who we can trust and who we want to "do life" with. Friendships are now very complicated.

I (Kristi) can remember as a teenager spending hours and hours at a time on the phone with my friends after school and on weekends. With my friends there was never a loss for words and never a shortage of excitement to talk about what was going on in my life. However, my parents complained that I never talked to them. Can you relate? Well, that happens for a reason. It is within our peer relationships that we learn how to expand our relational skills to the broader world. We practice communicating and dealing with conflict, and we develop the interpersonal skills needed in dating relationships. Even when our parents have done a good job of modeling these relational skills, we still need to "try them on for size." We do that best with our peers. Hopefully, we can go to our parents or another trusted adult for help when we get stuck or hurt but, ultimately, transferring these skills to our peer relationships is something that is required for our growth and maturity.

Knowing what we've just told you, doesn't it make sense now why your friends and peers are so important to you? They may even feel like your entire world. That's normal, but when there's great *need*, there's also great *risk*. When we need our friends to develop our relationship skills, we also are at risk of being wounded in the process. When our friends are our whole world, our peers have great power to hurt us. If we don't understand and respect the power of our words and actions, we can harm each other in deep ways. You must choose your friends carefully—your peer relationships can make or break you as a teenager or young adult.

When you go through life with unmet emotional and relational needs because of hurt in your family, you become more susceptible to accept inappropriate behavior from your friends and, eventually, the people you date. Of course, not everyone who reads this book will be in a dating relationship. That's okay—this information can apply to your friendships as well. Your friendships provide the foundation for dating anyway. So whether you're dating someone or not, we want you to read this chapter with an open mind. The more you can recognize unhealthy patterns in relationships, the better chance you'll have of avoiding some of these common pitfalls.

## Dating

My boyfriend's name is Manuel. He's nineteen years old. I really do love him. We have known each other for about five years, but we've been together for three years. I'm happy with him and everything. But on the other hand I'm not because he's too controlling and jealous. We always argue about stupid stuff. He always thinks that I'm doing something wrong and that hurts me. He's my everything. He's just getting too aggressive, and sometimes when he grabs me, he leaves bruises on me. I mean, if he keeps it up it's over between us. He doesn't mean to hurt me, but he does most of the time. We are always fighting.

– Paulina, age seventeen

Ms. Ickes,

I want to tell you something, but I'm embarrassed and don't want to say it to you in person. Remember how I told you how I got jumped a few weeks ago and had to miss so much school? Well, I lied. All those bruises and scratches on my face, neck, and arms were actually from my girlfriend. Sometimes we fight. She drinks a lot. I think her drinking makes it worse because it didn't used to be like this. When I try to tell her something, she gets mad real fast. I can't figure out what I'm doing wrong. I know it's wrong to hit girls. I do get mad, too, and I try to defend myself when she goes off on me but what else can I do? I don't want to hurt her. I love her. But it's embarrassing to come to school looking all messed up. Everyone will make fun of me if they find out I got beat up by a girl. But it's not like that. I could hurt her real bad if I wanted to, but she's not a dude—that's not right. She tells me she's sorry. If I can get her to come to school with me to see you, will you help us?

– Danny, age eighteen

While dating should be a context in which we grow and experience encouragement, healthy friendship, and love, all too often it involves abuse. Consider the following statistics.

One in five American high school girls report being physically or sexually assaulted by a male partner.[1]

One in three teens reports knowing a friend or peer who has been hit, punched, kicked, slapped, or physically hurt by a partner; and 45 percent of girls know a friend or peer who has been pressured into having either intercourse or oral sex.[2]

Two in five children between the ages of eleven and twelve report that their friends are victims of verbal abuse in relationships.[3]

With the way abuse gets "passed" from generation to generation, it shouldn't surprise us that so many people experience physical, sexual, verbal, or emotional abuse in a dating relationship. The abuse may happen once in a while or very frequently, even daily. And anyone can become involved with an abuser: both men and women can be victims, and it even happens in same-gender relationships.

Most of the time an abusive person doesn't show his or her true colors early in the relationship. In fact, an abusive dating partner may initially lavish attention, affection, gifts, and encouragement. As we saw in Paulina's story, her boyfriend Manuel set himself up to be her "everything." Because this attention met her emotional needs, it felt good and made it harder for her to identify how abusive his behavior was. This explains how a person could get into an abusive relationship: if you were treated badly, called names, or slapped on a first date, you wouldn't go on a second! Many times it's not until the relationship progresses that the abuse begins. There are, however, some warning signs that you can look for in friendships and early in dating.

Since many of us have grown up in families where we've seen conflict or divorce, it makes it hard to know what a healthy relationship looks like. The relationships we've grown up with seem to be "normal," because that's all we've ever known.

It's important that you learn the difference between healthy and unhealthy relationships so you don't repeat the same patterns. Take a look at the following characteristics in the chart on the next page and put a star next to any you've experienced in your relationships (include friendships as well as dating).[4] Then read the list a second time and circle any characteristics you see in your family. These could be characteristics you see in your biological parent, guardian, foster parent, stepparent, or your single parent's boyfriend or girlfriend.

HUSBANDS, LOVE YOUR WIVES, JUST AS CHRIST LOVED THE CHURCH AND GAVE HIMSELF UP FOR HER.... IN THIS SAME WAY, HUSBANDS OUGHT TO LOVE THEIR WIVES AS THEIR OWN BODIES. HE WHO LOVES HIS WIFE LOVES HIMSELF. AFTER ALL, NO ONE EVER HATED THEIR OWN BODY, BUT THEY FEED AND CARE FOR THEIR BODY, JUST AS CHRIST DOES THE CHURCH. (EPHESIANS 5:25, 28-29)

| In **UNHEALTHY** relationships: | In **HEALTHY** relationships: |
|---|---|
| ❑ One person makes all the decisions. | ❑ There is mutual respect (balanced power). |
| ❑ There is possessiveness, jealousy, controlling behavior. | ❑ There is trust and freedom to be who you are. |
| ❑ Feelings are not discussed. | ❑ There is open communication about feelings. |
| ❑ One partner ridicules and insults the other's feelings. | ❑ There is kindness, gentleness, and respect. |
| ❑ One person isolates the other from family/friends. | ❑ Time with family/friends is encouraged. |
| ❑ Parents don't know/don't approve of the relationship. | ❑ Parents know and approve of the relationship. |
| ❑ One person is 3+ years older (for teens). | ❑ Each person has a similar age/maturity level. |
| ❑ The guy talks/acts like girls are inferior to guys. | ❑ The guy values/respects girls for their gifts and abilities. |
| ❑ There are unpredictable/extreme mood changes. | ❑ There is emotional security and stability. |
| ❑ Anger is blamed on the partner. | ❑ Each person takes responsibility for his/her own anger. |
| ❑ One partner tempts the other to do wrong (ditch school, use drugs/alcohol, blow off homework, etc.). | ❑ Both partners are challenged to be their best (get along with parents, stay in school, make good choices, etc.). |
| ❑ One partner doesn't take no for an answer (going out, decisions, sex, etc.). | ❑ Both partners respect boundaries (you can't say yes and mean it unless you can also say no). |
| ❑ Anger is used to intimidate and manipulate to deal with conflict. | ❑ Respectful conversation is used to resolve conflict. |
| ❑ One/both partners are addicted. | ❑ No one is actively addicted. |
| ❑ One partner cheats on the other. | ❑ Each person stays committed to the relationship (no cheating). |
| ❑ One partner lies to parents, friends (is dishonest in general). | ❑ Both partners consistently tell the truth even about difficult things. |
| ❑ One partner is unable to admit being wrong. | ❑ Both partners take responsibility for wrong behavior without making excuses and blaming others. |
| ❑ There are double standards—expectations apply to only one person. | ❑ There are mutually agreed-upon expectations for the relationship (Do we date other people? etc.). |
| ❑ There is verbal, physical, or emotional abuse. | ❑ There is no verbal, physical, or emotional abuse. |

In a healthy relationship, both people are treated with equal importance. There's mutual respect and admiration between them. Both feel secure with who they are, and—while they may lean on each other for support—they're not dependent upon each other to be happy. A safe person is understanding, kind, and compassionate—even during times of anger and conflict. If a safe person *does* yell at you or hurt your feelings, he or she will later feel bad, sincerely apologize without blaming you, and take responsibility by learning to respond a different way the next time. In healthy relationships, both people strive to be their best and are encouraged by their partner to take risks and made decisions that will improve their lives. A safe person isn't threatened by his or her partner's success, but instead feels proud and is encouraging. We can't expect perfection because everyone makes mistakes, but we can *and should* expect to be treated with dignity and respect.

## AND LET US CONSIDER HOW WE MAY SPUR ONE ANOTHER ON TOWARD LOVE AND GOOD DEEDS. (HEBREWS 10:24)

My past is a painful one, and my relationship with my boyfriend has had its ups and downs. It's not perfect. But Rudy is showing me what it's like to have a guy love me and treat me with respect. At the beginning of our relationship (when I was sixteen), I had a habit of shutting down and holding in all of my feelings. I learned this habit from my family and the way my parents argued with each other. So when Rudy and I argued, I would get extremely mad and Rudy would have no clue why! But Rudy was both strong and gentle at the same time, and he helped me face my feelings. I remember one time we were driving in the car on the way to a movie, and I had tears streaming down my face. I can't even remember why now. Rudy asked me if I was okay and what was wrong. I said, "Nothing, I'm okay." Knowing that wasn't the truth, Rudy pulled the car over to the side of the road, stopped, and said, "I don't want to go into the movies when you're hurting like this. Can we please talk about it?" He sincerely wanted to listen to my thoughts and feelings and love me, including my emotions. It took his actions to show me how much he really cared. He's vocal at initiating painful discussions when he needs to, but sensitive when relating to me. He's strong and I feel protected by him, but he's also kind and loving. Rudy and I are determined to work through our problems right away when they're brought up, so they don't put distance between us. It's a lot of hard work! But man, am I thankful for it!

– Karen, age twenty

DON'T USE FOUL OR ABUSIVE LANGUAGE. LET EVERYTHING YOU SAY BE GOOD AND HELPFUL, SO THAT YOUR WORDS WILL BE AN ENCOURAGEMENT TO THOSE WHO HEAR THEM. ...

GET RID OF ALL BITTERNESS, RAGE, ANGER, HARSH WORDS, AND SLANDER, AS WELL AS ALL TYPES OF EVIL BEHAVIOR. INSTEAD, BE KIND TO EACH OTHER, TENDERHEARTED, FORGIVING ONE ANOTHER, JUST AS GOD THROUGH CHRIST HAS FORGIVEN YOU. (EPHESIANS 4:29, 31–32 NLT)

Today in my relationship with my girlfriend, if I feel like I have hurt her in any way, whether I feel like it's a big deal or not, I try to understand what I did and how I can fix it. It takes humility (which is something I have to work at every day because it doesn't come naturally) to go to her and ask what I did to hurt her. I have to be vulnerable before her, and when I do, she feels safe to tell me ways that I'm not meeting her needs. By seeking emotional openness in our relationship, I'm being a leader (which is exhibiting strength) in our relationship, while doing so with a clear gentleness. My girlfriend, as a result, vows not to shut down when she's hurt or when she's feeling a lot, but instead she feels safe enough to come to me. Each time we do this, we continue to add to our trust in one another, which strengthens our bond.

– Rudy, age twenty

THE WAY OF A FOOL SEEMS RIGHT TO HIM, BUT A WISE MAN LISTENS TO ADVICE. (PROVERBS 12:15)

A GENTLE ANSWER TURNS AWAY WRATH, BUT A HARSH WORD STIRS UP ANGER. (PROVERBS 15:1)

The following chart categorizes various abusive behaviors that often occur in dating relationships.

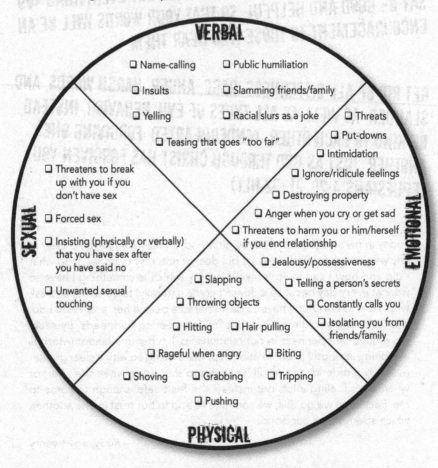

## What Has Shaped Our Views of Dating and Sex?

If you've grown up in the church and around Christians, you'll immediately have a hunch about where this discussion is going. Most of you expect us to tell you that the Bible says to wait until you're married to have sex. No surprise, right? While that is in fact the case, it's important that we take an honest look at this topic and discuss it candidly. When you understand what has shaped your view of dating and sex, you'll be able to make better choices in relationships and avoid unnecessary hurt in your life.

### THE CHURCH

So, if we're going to be blunt and honest about this topic, then how about we go first? Here's something you may not have learned in Sunday school. Studies have shown that evangelical youth begin having sex at a *younger* age than their liberal peers and are far *more* likely to have had three or more sexual partners than their nonevangelical peers (13.7 percent versus 8.9 percent).[5] What? Seriously? Keep reading because the information on *adults* is even more staggering. Research by the Barna Group on self-professed "born agains" found that there was no difference evident between born agains and "non-born agains" when it came to the likelihood of viewing pornography. Even though born agains were *twice* as likely not to go to a movie because of its rating, they were found to be *equally* likely as non-born agains to view pornography in secret.[6] Finally, when it comes to divorce, Christians divorce at rates similar to non-Christians.[7]

So here's the part of the conversation that perhaps you've never heard before. We Christians talk a good game when it comes to sexual morals and values, but we often do a terrible job of living out these principles in real life. We wonder if *that's* why some Christian teens are having sex *earlier* than their peers. Students are savvy and quickly notice that something isn't adding up. Well, you're right. As adults, we've done a bad job of giving you the full picture of *why* God gives us guidelines for our sexual behavior, and we *certainly* have done a bad job of teaching and modeling to you how to live that out. That's what we'd like to try and correct here.

Of course, not all Christians are hypocrites. Many practice what they preach in beautiful and sacrificial ways. Steve and Celestia work with many Christian couples and singles whose marriages and sexual behaviors are healthy, godly, and exemplary. The point in all of this is that the American church often isn't giving positive examples regarding sexuality and relationships. If you don't see positive examples, that can have a profoundly negative impact on your views of dating and sex. Maybe this has happened to you.

## THE INTERNET

Your generation has been exposed to more sexual information than any previous generation. You're the first group of young people to grow up exposed to the Internet all your lives. For the first time in our nation's history, information can be gathered instantly and anonymously from around the world. This has greatly affected your view of sex and relationships and has created new ways in which you're vulnerable to being abused and wounded.

One problem with the Internet is that it gives you a fake version of relationship. Meeting people online is very impersonal. It may have the appearance of real relationships, but people are kept at a distance, and you're never sure if who you're meeting online is who that person really is in real life. You're *seemingly* able to connect with others, but there's not real relationship. Couples can meet, develop their relationship, and break up—all online or by texting. As a result, it's difficult to learn how to develop real relational skills such as honesty, conflict resolution, and genuine mutual respect for one another. In fact, it's commonly stated that only 8 percent of communication comes from our mere words. That means that 92 percent of the messages we send and receive are interpreted through the filter of body language, tone of voice, and facial expression. We're at an extreme disadvantage when we communicate through email, texting, or online. Many times our conflicts are compounded by more hurt feelings and misunderstandings when the message is improperly conveyed.

The second issue with the Internet is pornography. A study of young adults found that the increase in the availability of pornography is changing our entire culture. Since pornography often pairs sex with violence, it teaches us that abuse is a normal part of sex and relationships. Porn promotes abuse because it removes the personal side of sex; programs guys to objectify and use women to satisfy their own needs; programs women to accept degrading behavior from men; and provides children, teens, and young adults with inaccurate and unhealthy sex education.

As many as 90 percent of boys and 70 percent of girls aged thirteen to fourteen have accessed sexually explicit content at least once.[8] The majority say that the first time they saw pornography, it happened innocently while they were doing online research for homework. It's not uncommon to experiment with pornography out of curiosity about sex. But then, it can be easy to get lured in and begin viewing pornography on a regular basis, even compulsively.

Continued use of pornography affects guys and girls in similar and yet slightly different ways. Over time, guys often become more violent sexually, are more dissatisfied with girls' bodies, and tend to be more selfish, aggressive, demeaning, impersonal, secretive, and dishonest. Girls who view pornography also become more sexually aggressive, are much more willing to accept casual sex from guys (friends with benefits, hooking up, oral sex, etc.), and are more likely to accept physical violence, sexual violence, and degrading forms of sex.[9]

It can be tempting to think that pornography is harmless and that it's something we can enjoy now and easily give up later. However, that's far from the case. The things that you do with your body and mind today automatically become cemented into your brain, heart, and soul. As a teen, your behaviors and choices can literally create pathways in your brain that become very difficult to change later in life. The things that you see and experience now will shape your view of sex and relationships and be the foundation you take into adulthood.

Our culture has tricked us into thinking that the view of sex seen in pornographic movies and websites is the norm. But the reality is that the images of sex seen online and in movies are catastrophically damaging. For instance, some of the most disturbing research studies on the effects of pornography were done with young men in college. Researchers found that after even a brief period of exposure to sexually violent pornography (roughly an hour a week for several weeks), young men were *twice* as likely to say that they would rape a woman if they knew they wouldn't get caught.[10] Not only can pornography impact us deeply, but it also can do it very quickly. One study showed significant, scientifically verifiable negative changes in guys' attitudes toward females after only *one fifteen-minute exposure* to pornography.[11]

If you're going to develop healthy gender relationships and build healthy sexuality, you must take seriously the dangers of pornography. If you're struggling with pornography, find a trusted godly adult you can talk to who can help you break this harmful habit. The *easiest* day to get help and quit is today. Each day you wait, the more you get lured in, and the more difficult it will be to stop.

## Creation, Gender, and Sex

First, it's important to understand that our sexuality isn't just about having sex. Our sexuality is about all the things that make up who we are as a guy (our masculinity) or a girl (our femininity). We're each different, and many times we're attracted to each other *because* of those differences. The qualities guys or girls have allow us to complement each other in how we think, feel, and act. Each of us must learn to express our strengths and have healthy, connected relationships with one another.

## SO GOD CREATED HUMAN BEINGS IN HIS OWN IMAGE.

### IN THE IMAGE OF GOD HE CREATED THEM;

#### MALE AND FEMALE HE CREATED THEM. (GENESIS 1:27 NLT)

Sometimes we wrongly assume that true masculinity is seen in the jock football player who likes cars, sports, and weightlifting, and who is tough and aggressive. We may also assume that true femininity is seen in the cheerleader who likes makeup and shopping, wears frilly skirts, and is sweet and passive. That's not what we mean. If so, then I (Kristi) am not very feminine because I don't identify with any of those "girly" characteristics. In fact, the majority of people don't fit into those narrow categories. We all have our own unique abilities, strengths, and personalities, so normal, healthy masculinity or femininity has a wide range of expression. Having said that, men and women are obviously different biologically and in other ways. Those differences are God-given and allow us to beautifully complement each other. In short, we need the opposite gender and they need us!

We do, however, want to note one biological gender difference that's very relevant to abuse. As a gender, males have more physical strength and are generally more physically and sexually aggressive, primarily because they have ten to twenty times more testosterone than females do. This helps to explain why even though males and females are equally sinful and can be equally unhealthy and abusive, males are much more likely to sexually assault females than females are likely to sexually assault males. While females can be physically aggressive, when it comes to domestic violence, females are much more likely to be physically injured than males are. For instance, 75 percent of the victims of violent family crimes are female.[12] For every one man hospitalized due to being assaulted by a female intimate partner, forty-six women are hospitalized due to being assaulted by a male partner.[13]

So guys sometimes *misuse* their strength to try and control and hurt others. But guys can also be committed to serve, speak up for, and protect their friends, families, and community (healthy masculinity). If guys everywhere would activate *healthy* masculinity, we would not have the social injustices and abuses of women and children that we see today.

In relationships when guys and girls can respectfully embrace their differences and appreciate each other as equals, great things happen; it's good for everyone. There are companies that require that a man and woman work together in teams. Corporate America knows that to be thorough, effective, and successful, there needs to be both men and women working together, each using their unique strengths for a common purpose.

We (Steve and Celestia) have found this to be such an important principle that we now do virtually all of our speaking and writing (including this book) with each other. Our personalities and gifts are very different, so we greatly benefit from working together.

When you're free to express your masculinity and femininity in relationships, have a regular amount of nonsexual physical touch, and emotionally connect with others, you experience confidence and strength in your life. These connections allow you to express your sexuality without having to be physically sexual. That's not to say that you won't feel physically attracted to someone or shouldn't express any physical affection. You just need to be careful not to be driven by sexual urges or buy into the lie that sex creates intimacy. God designed sex to be one of the most powerful *expressions* of committed (marital) love, but it doesn't *create* love or intimacy.

## God Loves You and Wants to Protect You and Provide for Your Deepest Needs

Many times people feel pressure to be sexually active even when there's a part of them that doesn't want to. In fact in one study, *one in four sexually active teens reported having intercourse when they really didn't want to.*[14] When you have sex too soon, it brings emotional pain into your life that can be avoided by waiting until marriage. It's important to think about how you'll maintain your sexual purity and boundaries *before* you're in a relationship. If you wait until you're dating someone, when all of your emotions are charged, it'll be more difficult to make a wise choice. So now is the time to think this through and make some commitments.

Think back to your first boyfriend or girlfriend. I (Kristi) had my first boyfriend in the seventh grade. I remember how exciting it was to hold his hand while we walked around school at recess. After going out for a few weeks, we broke up—I don't even remember being upset about it. As I've gotten older, I realize that the more physically involved we are with another person, the more we become attached, the more emotional pain we experience when it ends, and the harder it is for us to make wise relational decisions.

It's interesting that even when couples live together, research shows that, compared to married couples, those relationships have a much higher risk for domestic violence, infidelity, and breakups. Research shows that married couples feel more relationally close to one another and satisfied with their sex lives. Saving sex until marriage is God's ideal because marriage creates the most committed and secure environment a person can have.

God loves us so much that he gives us guidelines such as saving sex for marriage—not just because he said so, but because he knows that it really is best for us. It's pretty cool when secular research backs up biblical principles.[15] This certainly is one of those times. God knows that we will ultimately be more satisfied with our relationships, feel more intimacy, enjoy sex more, and be free from the consequences of sex too soon if we wait.

THE LORD WILL WITHHOLD NO GOOD THING FROM THOSE WHO DO WHAT IS RIGHT. (PSALM 84:11 NLT)

God made fire, and fire is good. It can cook food, keep us warm, and give us light. But what would happen if we took the fire from the fireplace and moved it to the living room rug? A lot of damage, right? It would get out of control and destroy everything in its path. In fact, we could even lose our lives. The fire itself isn't bad—it's the decision to take it out of the appropriate context that's bad. It's best to keep the fire in the fireplace where we can respect it for its destructive power and also enjoy it for all its benefits. The same is true with sex. God has given us the boundary of marriage for our protection and safety. In *that* context God himself says that sex is *very* good. Outside of that context it gets out of control and is destructive. Therefore, even though others may call us old-fashioned, we can trust the God who created sexuality and follow his commands for relationships.

It's very difficult to adhere to a biblical sexual ethic. In our culture, being sexually active is viewed as the norm and as an expectation for young singles. Virginity isn't something that's celebrated in our culture, but instead is seen as a reason to ridicule someone. We think of the movie *The 40-Year-Old Virgin*, which depicts the main character as a nerdy guy who "can't get any." Also, society views sexual restraint as an impossible task. Josh Hartnett plays a good-looking young man who vows to stay celibate in the movie *40 Days and 40 Nights*. The tagline for the movie was, "One man is about to do the unthinkable. No sex. Whatsoever. For… 40 Days and 40 Nights. Easy to say, harder to do." The movie depicts the decision to be abstinent for even forty days to be impractical for a young man living in a sexually charged society. In reality, it's not impossible to practice sexual self-control, nor is it unhealthy. Our culture has a very strange, illogical double standard when it comes to self-denial.

> We particularly affirm and handsomely reward athletes who abstain from sleep, food, physical comfort, and even medical care to get an Olympic gold medal, win the Tour de France, or climb Mount Everest. We recognize that when a greater good is in view, it is commendable, healthy, and beneficial to give up various physical pleasures. Our culture does not apply this same logic to sex, but it should. It is the Christian sexual ethic that is most logical and defensible…[God] asks singles to live out their sexuality [by] abstain[ing] from this physical pleasure for the greater good. For most, this will mean abstaining until marriage. For some who are called to a life of singleness, it will mean lifelong abstinence for the greater good of the kingdom of God. Jesus himself modeled this principle.[16]

Maybe one of the greatest responses singles can give as to the reason for choosing abstinence is to simply say, "I'm in training." If you're going to be able to withstand the sexual temptations that come *after* marriage (surprise—temptations *don't* go away when you get married), then you must practice having control over your body and sexual desires now. What a fantastic way to build trust with the person you will someday marry. Ultimately, if you know that your husband or wife learned and practiced the self-control needed to be abstinent *before* marriage, then how much more will you trust that person not to cheat on you *after* marriage?

We encourage you to talk about these principles with adults you trust. Ask questions. Expect honest answers. Then, focus on having healthy, non-sexual relationships with both guys and girls. Those healthy relationships, along with good accountability, prayer, and encouragement will give you the freedom and strength to say no. Our prayer for you is: "May God himself, the God of peace, sanctify you through and through. May your whole spirit, soul and body be kept blameless at the coming of our Lord Jesus Christ. The one who calls you is faithful and he will do it (1 Thessalonians 5:23–24).

My boyfriend and I decided that we will save sex for marriage only. It's a daily struggle, especially because having sex is almost expected at my high school. I've learned that I have to love and respect myself (my heart and my body) and believe that I'm worth waiting for. For me, when I desire sex, what I really want is love, security, tenderness, acceptance, and hope that the relationship will last. My boyfriend values all of those needs best by not having sex with me. That demonstrates to me that he loves me. Our relationship feels more safe and secure, he's tender toward me, he accepts me, and I know our relationship is going to last because we're spending our time communicating—not making out or sleeping together. To help our commitment, we go on group dates, we have a curfew and stick to it, we don't give each other massages, we don't stay out late at night together, and we always have a plan when we're together— we don't just "hang out" with nothing to do. A guy can wait! In fact, if a guy loves you then he'll be happy to wait.

– Kaylee, age eighteen

## Chapter Five Activities

### LEVEL ONE

Do you think most dating relationships are healthy or unhealthy? Why do you think teens and college students want to have a boyfriend or a girlfriend?

Do you think it's possible to save sex for marriage? Why or why not?

Think of a married couple you admire who are happily married. Ask them about the sexual and relational decisions they made while they were dating that positively contributed to their marital satisfaction today. What did you learn?

## LEVEL TWO

Reread the description of a healthy dating relationship on page 71. Write the name of anyone you've seen who has those characteristics.

Do you see any similarities between your dating relationships and your parents' relationship? How are they the same? How are they different?

What choices can/are you making in your dating relationships that will help you save sex until marriage?

## LEVEL THREE

Write a letter to yourself as a young guy or girl who's starting to think about dating. What would you tell yourself about dating and relationships? What commitments would you want to encourage yourself to make before starting this process? What advice would you give yourself about choosing the right person and expecting to be treated with respect?

Reread the letter you just wrote. Is there anything in there that you need to commit to apply to your life now?

Write out your personal guidelines for a significant friendship with the opposite sex. What are the characteristics you want in a guy or girl? What characteristics will you avoid in a guy or girl?

# PART THREE

# When You Hurt

I HAVE LEARNED NOW THAT
WHILE THOSE WHO SPEAK
ABOUT ONE'S MISERIES
USUALLY HURT, THOSE WHO
KEEP SILENCE HURT MORE.

—C. S. LEWIS

Chapter Six

# RISKY AND DANGEROUS BEHAVIOR

## SUICIDE

TWO OUT OF EVERY TEN TEENAGERS HAVE SERIOUSLY CONSIDERED SUICIDE AT SOME POINT IN THEIR LIVES. PERSONS AGES SEVEN TO SEVENTEEN ARE ABOUT AS LIKELY TO BE VICTIMS OF SUICIDE AS THEY ARE TO BE VICTIMS OF HOMICIDE. IN MOST STATES JUVENILE SUICIDES ARE MORE COMMON THAN JUVENILE HOMICIDES.[1]

## SEXUAL BEHAVIOR

NATIONWIDE, 46 PERCENT OF HIGH SCHOOL STUDENTS HAD HAD SEXUAL INTERCOURSE, AND 14 PERCENT OF STUDENTS HAD HAD SEXUAL INTERCOURSE WITH FOUR OR MORE PARTNERS DURING THEIR LIFETIME.[2]

90 PERCENT OF EIGHT-TO-SIXTEEN-YEAR OLDS HAVE VIEWED PORNOGRAPHY ONLINE, USUALLY FOR THE FIRST TIME INNOCENTLY WHILE DOING HOMEWORK, AND ONE OUT OF THREE VISITORS TO ADULT WEBSITES ARE NOW FEMALES.

## ALCOHOL

MORE THAN 75 PERCENT OF HIGH SCHOOL SENIORS SAID THEY HAD TRIED ALCOHOL. EVEN AMONG EIGHTH GRADERS, ALCOHOL USE WAS COMMON—TWO-THIRDS HAD TRIED IT. AMONG AMERICAN YOUTH AGES FOURTEEN TO SEVENTEEN, AN ESTIMATED 3.3 MILLION ARE CONSIDERED PROBLEM DRINKERS.[3]

## DRUGS

HALF OF HIGH SCHOOL SENIORS (51 PERCENT) SURVEYED IN 2003 SAID THEY HAD TRIED ILLICIT DRUGS AT LEAST ONCE. HALF OF THOSE STUDENTS REPORT THAT THEY HAVE ALSO USED OTHER, HARDER DRUGS.[4]

## Why Am I Doing This? Is There Something Wrong with Me?

My family stinks. I will never forgive them. They chose to believe my mom's boyfriend and not me. They say I wanted attention and was trying to break them up. They only acted like they cared because they had to. We went to the police but nothing happened to him. The policeman told my mom not to let him near me because it was too dangerous. I felt so bad after this . . . like I felt mad, sad, and confused. I went through so many emotions, but it lasted only a few weeks. Then I found something that took all the pain away. I felt invincible, but it got out of control and I got sick. I even had to go to the hospital, but I got some help there.

A couple months later, I woke up and there he was again. My mom said that he was sorry and that she needed him. He moved back in like it was cool. She chose her happiness before my safety. I didn't feel safe but I wouldn't show it . . . that's exactly what he wanted. I kinda started to be a rebel. I would ditch school and just hang out. But I know lots of kids go through something like this. My best friend went through the same thing. I think that's why we're so close. I liked acting out. It was fun. And my mom didn't care. She was out partying just as much as me.

– Monique, age fifteen

Every day I (Kristi) talk with students who don't understand why they're doing things they know are unsafe or wrong. Many of them tell me the truth about their behavior and then feel embarrassed and ask me what's wrong with them. They feel that they are bad and that they'll be rejected if anyone else knew what they were doing. The more I hear students' stories, the more I understand why. Any negative behaviors or attitudes you have in your life are there for a reason. I've never met with any student who's said, "When I grow up, I want to be an alcoholic" or "One of my goals this school year is to get so depressed I'll think about killing myself." These behaviors stem from pain, and until that pain is healed, the behaviors continue and even intensify.

God designed families—and specifically parents—to meet physical, social, emotional, and spiritual needs. It's important to grow up feeling loved, enjoyed, and supported in a way that allows you to mess up and be honest about your struggles and temptations. Your parents are supposed to help you understand your emotions, dating, sex, how to deal with conflict, and many other things. Parents should be safe enough to let you talk through your problems, listen to you, and help you navigate life. Parents are also supposed to give you rules, limitations, and discipline. Even if we hate to admit it, we all want and need to have that kind of structure in our lives. When those needs are not met because of abuse or abandonment, the needs don't go away.

Pain can lead you to act out in the ways we mentioned at the beginning of this chapter. It's important to understand that there's a reason you're struggling with your behavior and the problems it has caused. Hidden under your behavior is an unmet need that's demanding to be met. Here are some examples of needs:

*Physical needs:* nutritious food, water, adequate shelter, weather-appropriate clothing, safety from harm, medical/dental care, appropriate physical touch/affection, exercise/activity.

*Emotional needs:* love, acceptance, connection with peers/adults, nurturing, affirmation, encouragement, self-definition (having a sense of who we are), a feeling of being bonded/close to others.

*Social needs:* interaction with peers and adults, a feeling of being important to a group or a greater cause, boundaries (the ability to tell someone no).

*Mental needs:* a feeling that we're good at something, opportunities to decide what's right/wrong in the world, the freedom to express oneself creatively through music, art, dance, etc.

If the above needs aren't met in healthy ways, we sometimes use unhealthy ways to meet them. One example is the physical need for food. At the beginning of chapter three, you read about a student who, because of her mom's abandonment, didn't have the food she needed. As a child she didn't have a healthy way to meet that need since she couldn't go out and get a job to pay for her food. Therefore, we can understand why she resorted to stealing food in order to eat. A risky behavior met her physical need. But since stealing is wrong and carries some big consequences, it wasn't the right way to meet that need.

Where do our needs come from? We have these needs because we're made in God's image. In the creation account in Genesis, it says that of all of creation, only humans are made in God's image. That's what gives us unique value, significance, and ability. The "image of God" involves all of the ways we're uniquely like God. For instance, we have the ability to communicate with language, we can use logic and reason, and we have the capacity to use our strengths and abilities to impact our world because God said, "Have dominion." Therefore, we long to have adventure and make a significant impact (make a difference) in the world. We long for intimacy and sexual fulfillment because God said "be fruitful and multiply."

The "image of God" particularly involves the ability and longing for intimate relationships. It can be hard to think that you need other people. When you've been hurt by others, you can become shut off to relationships and convince yourself that you can take care of everything on your own. Therefore, it's important to think about the need for relationships coming from God himself. If anyone could operate completely independent of others, it would be God. After all, he's God. But God is actually in a love relationship with himself (Father, Son, Holy Spirit). He doesn't operate alone. God needs others. So do you.

I [JESUS] PRAY THAT THEY WILL ALL BE ONE, JUST AS YOU AND I ARE ONE—AS YOU ARE IN ME, FATHER, AND I AM IN YOU. AND MAY THEY BE IN US SO THAT THE WORLD WILL BELIEVE YOU SENT ME.... I AM IN THEM AND YOU ARE IN ME. MAY THEY EXPERIENCE SUCH PERFECT UNITY THAT THE WORLD WILL KNOW THAT YOU SENT ME AND THAT YOU LOVE THEM AS MUCH AS YOU LOVE ME...THEN THEY CAN SEE ALL THE GLORY YOU GAVE ME BECAUSE YOU LOVED ME EVEN BEFORE THE WORLD BEGAN! (JOHN 17:21, 23–24 NLT)

When God made humans in his image, he specifically created us as a pair (a man and a woman). He didn't create us as isolated individuals meant to be complete on our own. He created us to need one another—

to fill gaps in each other to fully show who God is. We're meant for relationships. Therefore, our desire for relationships and the sexual longings that spring from them good and made by God.

So if our human longings are good and God-like, why do they seem to get us in so much trouble? The answer: Satan wants to destroy God's plan, and he's been at this evil scheme since the beginning. God made Adam and Eve and put them in a perfect place: the garden of Eden where all their needs were met. They had a need and a longing for food, so God gave them plenty of nutritious, luscious, tasty fruit to meet their needs. But Satan, the evil liar, came along and tried to hijack their God-given need by seducing them to satisfy their longing in an inappropriate and harmful way. Satan pointed out the *one* fruit that God said not to eat. He convinced them that the best way to meet their needs would be to eat the forbidden fruit. They bought the lie, ate, and experienced shame, guilt, isolation, and death.

The problem wasn't the need that Adam and Eve had for food. The problem was that Satan convinced them to meet that legitimate need in a way God said not to. There would be no reason for Adam and Eve to feel embarrassed that they were hungry. The hunger is okay. It *wasn't* okay how they tried to meet the need apart from God.

Today, Satan still hijacks our needs so that we try to meet them in ways that may seem to work, but actually will eventually destroy us. John 10:10 says, "The thief comes only to steal and kill and destroy; I [Jesus] have come that they may have life, and have it to the full." When we have unmet needs, there will be a powerful pull to meet those needs in unhealthy ways. We begin to feel shame over having the need in the first place, so we stop knowing how to look for healthy solutions to meet these needs. We don't ask others for help or talk about our feelings of emptiness or loneliness. We're embarrassed that we even need those things. Therefore, Satan can use that time of vulnerability to strike and trick us into meeting God-given needs in ways that will trap and eventually harm us.

You can see this dynamic at work in a teenage girl who has grown up without any love or affection from her father. She has not had her emotional needs met for love. Then she learns that she can get attention from guys by dressing in sexual ways and behaving sexually. This creates new pain and consequences in her life. The problem wasn't that she longed to be loved and cared for—the problem was that Satan tricked her into meeting that healthy need in an unhealthy way.

Let's see some more examples of Satan's plan in other risky behaviors:

| Behaviors: | Needs: |
|---|---|
| Sex | Physical touch, love, physical activity, emotional connection with peer(s), older boyfriend as a "father" substitute, feel desired/wanted/valuable, feeling close to someone |
| Partying | Social connection with peers, acceptance, a place to belong, having fun |
| Gang Involvement | Feeling important to a group or cause greater than ourselves, structure and clear limits, self-definition, sense of power |
| Graffiti | Creative expression, feeling good at something, being accepted by a group of peers, being seen/noticed |
| Pornography | Feeling of affection/bonding in a "safe" way, feeling good about one's body as a male/female, sexual excitement/pleasure |

When a need is met through a risky behavior, it's more difficult to stop that behavior and it's possible to get stuck. One person may experiment with those behaviors, experience some painful consequences, and be able to walk away having learned his lesson. For a person who has holes in his or her soul caused by unmet needs, pain, and abuse, these behaviors seem to fill up the holes, and the consequences aren't enough of a reason to stop. In reality, the behaviors are only a superficial and temporary solution that cause more pain and damage in the end.

One Memorial Day, I (Steve) watched an incredible interview with a man who had served in the U.S. Navy in World War II. His ship was torpedoed and sunk in the Pacific Ocean. He, along with hundreds of other sailors, escaped the doomed vessel by jumping into the ocean. After a day of bobbing in the water and sweltering in the tropical heat, a few of the men were so desperately thirsty that they decided to drink the seawater. Their buddies begged them to stop, to hang on until a rescue ship arrived with fresh water. But they were insane with thirst and drank their fill of salty water. They initially declared that the water was satisfying and encouraged the other sailors to give it a try. They didn't realize that within minutes of drinking the seawater, their bodies became much more dehydrated. Thus, drinking seawater actually made them thirstier. So over the next few hours, they drank more. By the end of the day they were dead, even though they had been drinking water all day.

It's terribly tragic that the men's misguided attempt to meet their own needs actually made the needs worse and ultimately destroyed them. This story demonstrates how the more intense our needs, the more desperate our attempts become to meet them, often in illegitimate, destructive ways. We, like the sailors, must wait for rescue. We must wait for God to provide for our needs in healthy ways.

## We Get Stuck Because of Intense Needs

If what we're saying is true, we should be able to find that people who are "stuck" doing these risky behaviors often have a history of some sort of deep pain or abuse that has intensified their God-given needs. This pain can also create a desire to numb the pain and unmet needs. Well, here's what we found:

NEGLECT [WAS] THE MOST POWERFUL PREDICTOR OF SELF-DESTRUCTIVE BEHAVIOR. THOSE ... WHO COULD NOT REMEMBER FEELING SPECIAL OR LOVED BY ANYONE AS CHILDREN WERE LEAST ABLE TO ... CONTROL THEIR SELF-DESTRUCTIVE BEHAVIOR.[5]

MORE THAN 70 PERCENT OF GIRLS IN THE JUVENILE JUSTICE SYSTEM HAVE HISTORIES OF ABUSE.[6]

ONE-HALF TO TWO-THIRDS OF TEEN MOTHERS WERE SEXUALLY MOLESTED PRIOR TO THEIR FIRST PREGNANCY.[7]

75 PERCENT OF PROSTITUTES ATTRIBUTED THEIR DECISION TO ENGAGE IN PROSTITUTION TO PAST SEXUAL ABUSE.[8]

THE MAJORITY OF TEENS WHO ENTER DRUG/ALCOHOL TREATMENT REPORT HAVING BEEN ABUSED.[9]

50 PERCENT OF PEOPLE WITH EATING DISORDERS EXPERIENCED CHILDHOOD ABUSE/NEGLECT.[10]

It's also important to note that even if you were not *directly* abused, *witnessing* violence or abuse produces some of the same effects on your behavior and relationships. Witnessing violence is connected to lifelong physical, emotional, and psychological problems; substance abuse; and being either the perpetrator or victim of an abusive relationship as an adult.[11]

> What some people don't understand is that domestic violence is bad, but watching domestic violence as a child is much worse. The images never erase. It always stays in the mind.
>
> – Ana, age thirteen

You may be reading this book because something is going on in your life that concerns you or has gotten out of control. Whatever the behavior—eating disorders, pornography, masturbation, sex, violence, drugs, alcohol, cutting, gang involvement, getting bad grades in school, or being on probation—now's the time to deal with it. Let us give you an example:

Do you ever get weeds in your backyard? I know I (Kristi) do. I think weeds are ugly. I'm a bit of a perfectionist and don't like an ugly yard. Do your parents ever make you go out and get rid of the weeds? I know mine did, and now that I'm a full-fledged adult I have the honor of doing it at my own house. As a teenager I remember wanting to get this awful chore done as quickly and easily as possible. I had more important, fun things to do. So I had a brilliant idea. I got a pair of scissors, and I went into the backyard and cut off all the weeds right at the bottom. It took only fifteen minutes for me to do the entire yard. I felt that I was a genius and my parents would never know the difference. About a week later I came home from school, and my mom was mad. The weeds had grown back and she knew I had taken the easy way out.

I suggested to my mom that we just close the blinds on the patio door so we'd never have to see those weeds again, and then I could go out with my friends that night. (Apparently, I wasn't real bright back then.) I thought she was going to explode! To make a long story short, I missed the movie with my friends, and I had to get on my hands and knees and spend an hour and a half digging out those weeds the right way, root and all.

Why do I share such a random story from my childhood? Because that's the same mistake that adults often make with teens. We see some behaviors (weeds) in your life that are ugly, and we want a quick fix. We either turn the blinds on the patio door and act like the problems aren't there, or we try to chop them off. We ground you or yell at you to try and stop the behaviors, but that doesn't get to the root of the problem. As adults, we sometimes want a quick fix, and we don't want to go through all the hard work of digging into your life to find the root causes of the problems we see. I'm sorry on behalf of so many adults who aren't willing (or don't know how) to help you get to the bottom of your struggles. God sees and knows what your heart needs, and he is committed to your growth and healing. So let's commit to continuing this hard work together.

ON THAT DAY
THEY WILL SAY TO JERUSALEM,
"DO NOT FEAR, O ZION;
DO NOT LET YOUR HANDS HANG LIMP.
THE LORD YOUR GOD IS WITH YOU,
THE MIGHTY WARRIOR WHO SAVES.
HE WILL TAKE GREAT DELIGHT IN YOU,
IN HIS LOVE HE WILL NO LONGER REBUKE YOU,
BUT WILL REJOICE OVER YOU WITH SINGING."
(ZEPHANIAH 3:16-17)

We're so proud of you for reading this far. We promise that if you're willing to connect your struggles to your past hurts, you *will* find answers. Then, as your hurts are healed and you're able to have healthy relationships, your needs will be met in the way God designed. You'll feel hopeful, alive, and empowered to stop your behaviors because you won't need them anymore. So again, we want to encourage you: Don't stop reading here. Keep going. Answer the questions at the end of each chapter. Share your answers with an adult, friend, or small group of people who you trust. Find healing by allowing God to meet your needs in a healthy way.

BEING CONFIDENT OF THIS, THAT HE WHO BEGAN A GOOD WORK IN YOU WILL CARRY IT ON TO COMPLETION UNTIL THE DAY OF CHRIST JESUS. (PHILIPPIANS 1:6)

## Chapter Six Activities

### LEVEL ONE
What risky or negative behaviors have you experimented with?

What in your life would you like to see changed as a result of working through this book?

## LEVEL TWO

Make a list of risky or negative behaviors you are struggling with (or have struggled with in the past). Next to each one, list the need that the behavior could be meeting.

Behaviors:                    Needs:

## LEVEL THREE

Go back to your timeline on page 41 and add any risky behaviors (write or draw them in a different color).

Do your behaviors connect/start/end with other significant events in your life? Write about any connections you make.

## Chapter Seven

# GUILT AND SHAME

I still feel it was my fault. I only lived with my dad for about a year (when I was thirteen). When I moved back into my mother's house, the sexual abuse continued right where it left off. My only real escape was through music and video games. I only had one friend, and I think his parents sensed something was wrong with me since they constantly invited me places and tried to keep me away from my house. I started dating a girl, and it was a good time to be with her; but for the majority of the relationship, I never really opened up to her. To be honest, I've never fully opened up to anyone other than writing this paper. To this day I still feel everything that happened to me was my fault, and for almost a year, I would cut myself. I suppose the pain made me feel I was erasing all of the shame and guilt I felt, but it never worked.

The final straw for me was one Christmas when my mom, the only person I ever felt loved me, left without telling anyone. It made me feel as though she didn't want me in her life and would rather be with her boyfriend. That day I started drinking and it seemed the drinking never stopped. I drank every single chance I got, sometimes up to four times a week. It was the only time I ever felt good about myself. The only time I was happy was when I was drunk. It continued for the longest time and no one seemed to care. I drank and drank, not caring about the consequences, not caring who I hurt. I'm not even sure what compelled me to stop, but I just figured it was time to change my life.

– Gabe, age sixteen

Let's set aside the topic of abuse for a moment and talk about an emotion called shame. Shame is the most powerful human emotion, and just like a superhero's superhuman strength, that power can be used for good or for evil. There are two types: healthy shame and unhealthy (toxic) shame.

# Healthy Shame Is Guilt

Guilt is the feeling we get when we do something wrong. Because we're made in God's image, all human beings have a conscience: that inner voice that whispers—or sometimes shouts—that we've done something wrong, that we're guilty. God gives us that emotion because he loves us and, like a healthy parent, wants to gently correct us and protect us from the damaging consequences of sin. We *should* feel (healthy) shame when we hit our younger sibling and make her cry; get caught cheating on an exam and risk getting an F for the course; sneak out of the house and get drunk at a party. Things we do that are wrong *should* cause us emotional discomfort. That feeling is our warning sign that we've sinned and need to make things right with God and others. If we listen to this feeling, we'll repent and change our behavior. While guilt is a painful emotion, it's important to pay attention to it because it's God's gift to us to encourage and motivate us to make positive changes in our lives.

I AM NOT SORRY THAT I SENT THAT SEVERE LETTER TO YOU, THOUGH I WAS SORRY AT FIRST, FOR I KNOW IT WAS PAINFUL TO YOU FOR A LITTLE WHILE. NOW I AM GLAD I SENT IT, NOT BECAUSE IT HURT YOU, BUT BECAUSE THE PAIN CAUSED YOU TO REPENT AND CHANGE YOUR WAYS. IT WAS THE KIND OF SORROW GOD WANTS HIS PEOPLE TO HAVE, SO YOU WERE NOT HARMED BY US IN ANY WAY. FOR THE KIND OF SORROW GOD WANTS US TO EXPERIENCE LEADS US AWAY FROM SIN AND RESULTS IN SALVATION. THERE'S NO REGRET FOR THAT KIND OF SORROW. BUT WORLDLY SORROW, WHICH LACKS REPENTANCE, RESULTS IN SPIRITUAL DEATH. (2 CORINTHIANS 7:8–10 NLT)

In 2 Corinthians 7:8–10, Paul tells the church in Corinth about the difference between guilt and shame. He explains that both feelings bring pain, but when that pain causes us to "repent and change our ways" then it's a good kind of pain and it's something that God wants us to experience because it leads us away from sin and closer to him. There he's talking about guilt. Paul goes on, however, to say that the pain that comes from the *world* is not the good kind of pain. It leads us *away* from God. There he's referring to shame—we'll talk about that later in the chapter.

## Guilt Keeps Us "In the Fish Bowl"

My (Kristi's) first pets were two goldfish named Fred and Fanny (don't ask me why). I got them in first grade at a school carnival. I took them home in a baggy, and my parents bought me one of those octagon-shaped bowls with little rocks, fake plants, and everything.

As a six-year-old I understood something very important: My fish needed to stay in their bowl. I didn't understand the science of how fish got oxygen from the water, but I knew they needed to stay in the bowl. What was interesting about these two fish is that they had a tendency to pop their heads out of the water, as if they were trying to jump out. I can only imagine the conversations going on between them:

"Fred, I'm sick of this stupid bowl. There's hardly any room in here."

"I know what you mean, Fanny. Look at all the space out there!"

"Are you thinking what I'm thinking?"

"Yep ... let's get out of here!!"

So late one night, when everyone was asleep, it was time for their move. They swam around and around gathering up as much speed as possible and jumped out of the bowl. What do you think I found when I woke up the next morning? Two dead fish on the table. Now, don't feel too bad for me—I was six, and I eventually got over it (they were only fish, you know). But I really do wish they could have understood that the boundary of their fish bowl was there for their own good. Sure, it looked big, free, and fun on the outside; but the truth was that what they thought would bring them freedom brought them only death.

You're a lot like those two fish. God has given you boundaries and rules that govern your lives. Many times (and this is true for adults as well) you look beyond those boundaries and think you're missing out on all the fun, freedom, and excitement. Since God loves you, he corrects you when you step outside his *protective* boundaries. One of the ways you experience correction is through feelings of guilt. The good news is that no matter how much you've sinned or gotten away from the fish bowl, God doesn't slap you back into place harshly. Guilt is God's gracious call to turn around and fix what you're doing. It's loving and gentle if you're willing to listen.

DO NOT LET YOUR HEART ENVY SINNERS, BUT ALWAYS BE ZEALOUS FOR THE FEAR OF THE LORD. (PROVERBS 23:17)

## Unhealthy Shame Is Toxic

Unhealthy shame, or "toxic shame," is a different story. *Toxic shame* is defined as a deep, painful feeling of not being good enough because you've failed to live up to an expectation—either a personal expectation or the expectations of others.[1] Here's the difference: Guilt causes you to say, "I did something wrong, I need to take responsibility and work on that." Toxic shame causes you to conclude that, "I'm totally messed up. There's no hope for me. I'm giving up."

"LET US LIE DOWN IN OUR [GUILT],
AND LET OUR DISGRACE COVER US.
WE HAVE SINNED AGAINST THE LORD OUR GOD,
BOTH WE AND OUR FATHERS;
FROM OUR YOUTH TILL THIS DAY
WE HAVE NOT OBEYED THE LORD OUR GOD"
"...O ISRAEL,
RETURN TO ME," DECLARES THE LORD.
(JEREMIAH 3:25–4:1 NIV 1984)

When you experience toxic shame, you feel a sense of disgust toward yourself and you want to hide from God and others. Toxic shame causes you to believe that if other people found out who you really are, they would reject and abandon you. Toxic shame causes isolation and is very destructive. There's no change of behavior and no adjustment of your life—there's only paralyzing pain and an avoidance of your true self, relationships with others, and God. Toxic shame distorts reality by going *beyond* convincing you that you've done bad *things* that need to be forgiven. It whispers to you that *you're* bad and unforgivable. Instead of pointing out the consequences of your choices, toxic shame distorts your view of yourself and your mistakes and makes you want to hide. Even when you really *have* done something wrong, toxic shame interprets your mistakes in a twisted way and strips you of hope. Toxic shame does *not* come from God. It is evil.

## The Lens of Toxic Shame

Shame is a powerful human emotion because once toxic shame enters your life, it confuses everything. Shame is like a virus invading a hard drive. It twists and distorts all of your experiences and feelings until it becomes very hard to remember what guilt feels like, much less how to respond to it. Sometimes you may feel toxic shame over a very minor mistake. Other times you may do something *really* bad and not feel guilty at all.

Have you ever gone to a 3-D movie? When you go to a 3-D movie, everyone wears plastic glasses that make the movie seem more real and much more scary. The only way 3-D movies are effective is if you wear the glasses. Taking off the glasses allows you to see the movie as it really is, which isn't very intense at all. Toxic shame works in a similar way. If you walk around seeing the world through the lenses of shame, it makes you see things differently than they really are. It makes situations and experiences seem more intense and scary, and it distorts your view of yourself—making you feel intense toxic shame when you aren't actually guilty, or little or no shame when you are. Life is very confusing and painful when you're wearing the lenses of toxic shame.

## Shame and Abuse

Remember earlier when we talked about how abusers blame others for their abusive actions? Well, here's where this ties in. An abuser should feel an immense amount of *guilt* for what he is doing (or has done). That guilt should result in so much pain that the abuser is broken with sorrow, repents, and takes responsibility for his actions. Instead, though, what does an abuser do? An abuser blames, judges, tricks, and intimidates the victim. But *someone* must feel the guilt because feelings don't just evaporate into thin air. So the abuser hands his guilt to the victim. Since the victim didn't do anything wrong, he or she *isn't guilty* but instead feels toxic *shame*. Then, because of the shame, the victim feels defective, bad, and disgusting, and wants to hide. Since the feelings of guilt and shame are similar, victims often think they *did* do something wrong even when they didn't. They're carrying the guilt and shame that belongs to the abuser.

In the Bible the prophet Jeremiah speaks a lot about guilt and shame. God repeatedly gives Israel opportunities to repent through the feeling of guilt. However, there were abusers among them who refused to listen to God's call to repentance. Notice the strong language in the following verses from Jeremiah chapters 5 and 6:

"Among my people are the wicked
who lie in wait like men who snare birds
and like those who set traps to catch people.
Like cages full of birds,
their houses are full of deceit;
they have become rich and powerful
and have grown fat and sleek.
Their evil deeds have no limit;
they do not promote the case of the fatherless;
they do not defend the just cause of the poor."

Should I not punish them for this?"
declares the LORD. (Jeremiah 5:26–29)

"Are they ashamed of their detestable conduct?
No, they have no shame at all;
they do not even know how to blush.
So they will fall among the fallen;
they will be brought down when I punish them,"
says the LORD. (Jeremiah 6:15)

These were abusers who were oppressing the poor and vulnerable. Sadly, they were so hardhearted that they were able to victimize orphans, widows, and the poor as if these innocent people were animals to be trapped, stripped, and disposed of. These abusers should have been overwhelmed with feelings of guilt, yet they put those feelings on their victims so they could hold their heads high—they didn't even blush over their disgraceful behavior. As you can see, God wasn't fooled, and he promised eventually to punish these unrepentant abusers.

In her song "I'm OK," Christina Aguilera says,

I often wonder why I carry all this guilt
When it's you that helped me put up all these walls I've built ...
Bruises fade, Father, but the pain remains the same.[2]

– Christina Aguilera (2002)

Christina Aguilera is correct that the pain of the abuse will stay with her *long* after the physical bruises fade. She describes how easy it is for abuse victims to take on the guilt of their abuser. The first reason that an abuser's shame sticks to the victim very easily is because it can be too painful to admit that someone who should have cared for you was the one who harmed you. The second reason is because, as we discussed in the last chapter, shame causes a person to become susceptible to shameful, risky behavior. You can begin living life outside the fish bowl and trying to cope with your pain. These risky behaviors produce guilt, but since you're wearing the lenses of toxic shame, you may feel you're too messed up to be forgiven—all bets are off and the new shame just confirms that something is wrong with you and that the abuse was your fault in the first place. What a mess!

## THE SHAME CYCLE: JESSICA'S STORY
Jessica's story demonstrates the incredible damage and confusion created by abuse and the resulting shame that leads to risky behavior. Jessica was a fifteen-year-old girl who'd been in and out of the juvenile detention center for various offenses like drug use, assault, and even prostitution. She'd long since dropped out of school, so the only time she

received an education was when she was in jail. In case you don't know how it works in juvenile detention facilities, teens attend school as a part of their sentence. They have certified teachers who work at the facilities, and they can earn middle school and high school credits.

Jessica's interactions with the detention schoolteachers seemed to be anything but beneficial. Even though the school staff was more understanding and compassionate than the detention guards, she was very angry and frequently got kicked out of her classes and sent back to her unit. After two years of being in and out of this facility, on the day Jessica was released, a teacher found the following note from her:

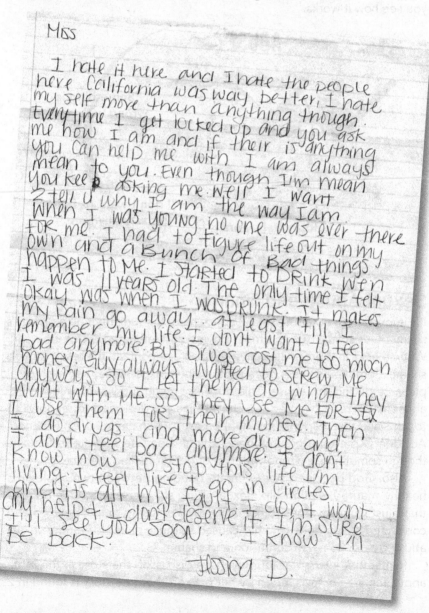

Miss

I hate it here and I hate the people here California was way better, I hate my self more than anything though. Everytime I get locked up and you ask me how I am and if their is anything you can help me with I am always mean to you. Even though I'm mean you keep asking me. Well I want 2 tell u why I am the way I am. When I was young no one was ever there for me. I had to figure life out on my own and a bunch of Bad things happen to Me. I started to DRink Wen I was 11 years old. The only time I felt okay was when I was DRUNK. It makes my pain go away. at least till I remember my life. I dont want to feel bad anymore. But Drugs cost me too much money. Guy always wanted to screw me anyways so I let them do what they want with me. So they use Me FOR SEX I use them FOR their money. Then I do drugs. and more drugs and I dont feel bad anymore. I dont know how to stop this life I'm living. I feel like I go in circles and its all my fault I don't want any help+ I dont deserve it. I'm SURE I'll see you soon    I know I'll be back.

Jessica D.

Sadly, the teacher never saw Jessica again and never learned why. Maybe Jessica turned eighteen and was sent to adult jail, or perhaps something more tragic happened. What we can learn from Jessica is about the shame cycle: Abuse makes you decide, "Something is wrong with me," which makes you say, "I don't want to feel this way anymore," which drives you to try to escape the pain by engaging in risky behaviors, which creates a lot of appropriate guilt. However, when you see through the lenses of toxic shame, you feel worthless and unworthy of forgiveness. That seems to confirm to you that something really is wrong with you and sets the cycle into motion again. The following picture will help you see how it works.

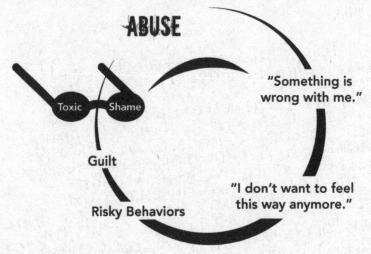

## Sexual Abuse and Shame

It's important to note that sexual abuse has a unique effect on a person's shame. Our sexuality is the most private and intimate part of a person. When there's inappropriate sexual exposure or contact, the result is deep shame. Sometimes this is because the victim experiences some physical pleasure during the abuse. This *does not* mean the victim enjoyed the abuse or secretly "wanted it." Our bodies are designed to respond to touch—and that response can happen *even when the touch isn't wanted.* Accidental pleasure creates deep shame because the victim feels as though something is wrong with him or her for feeling that way.

Also, God designed sex to create bonding between two adults in a healthy, married relationship. Sexual abuse still creates a unique bond—that's just what sex does to humans. How confusing to feel bonded and connected to someone who has caused so much pain. No wonder sexual abuse creates so much confusion and shame!

Remember in chapter four when we discussed the story in the Bible about Tamar? She was raped by her own brother (the story is found in 2

Samuel 13 if you want to reread it). Before Tamar's brother raped her, she said, "No, my brother! Don't be foolish! Don't do this to me! Such wicked things aren't done in Israel. Where could I go in my shame?"

Now that we've read the story, we know he didn't listen to her. Immediately after raping her, his "love turned to hate, and he hated her even more than he had loved her. 'Get out of here!' he snarled at her" (NLT).

Sadly, Tamar hadn't done anything wrong, but every time her brother looked at her, he was reminded of what he did and felt guilty. As a result, he blamed her and she carried the full weight of his guilt, which she experienced as shame. It's easy to understand that she was crushed by her rapist's shame—it wasn't hers to carry.

Shame has the greatest effect on your adjustment after the abuse. The grip of shame can be felt long after the abuse has stopped, which is confusing. Therefore, shame has to be addressed so God can expose it and heal it. We're going to look at a list to help you see how much you're struggling with toxic shame. Then we'll give you three steps to start the process of healing the shame in your life.

> THOSE WHO LOOK TO HIM ARE RADIANT;
> THEIR FACES ARE NEVER COVERED WITH SHAME.
> (PSALM 34:5)

# COMMON STATEMENTS MADE BY A SHAME-FILLED PERSON:
(check off any that you can relate to)

- ☐ "I'm not good enough. I don't deserve to be loved, something's wrong with me."
- ☐ "Things will never get better in my life. Why keep trying?"
- ☐ "I hate when others act like they're all that. What? Do they think they're better than me?"
- ☐ "I have to win in all circumstances. Sometimes people won't compete with me 'cause they say I'm a sore loser. Well, that's their problem. I'm just intense!"
- ☐ "When I make a mistake, I feel like a loser. I'll do what it takes to either be perfect...or at least make sure others see me that way!"
- ☐ "It's not my fault that things fell apart...it's all these other people."
- ☐ "No one understands me. I just don't fit in anywhere. Something must be wrong with me."
- ☐ "No one can know the real me. I have to keep it all together on the outside...otherwise no one will love me or accept me."
- ☐ "Sometimes I use too much alcohol, sex (or pornography), food...I just can't seem to get control of that area of my life. I guess that helps me feel better and not feel so much pain."
- ☐ "I just can't seem to make my relationships work. I can have casual friends or go on a few casual dates, but when it starts to get serious, it just doesn't work out. I guess I just want to have fun."
- ☐ "I have a lot of people that I don't like. But it's not my fault. People are just idiots!"
- ☐ "Most of the time I don't feel much of anything. And when I do, I'm not sure what it is."
- ☐ "I'm always tired. I have to keep myself busy but I don't know why."

## Healing Shame

Healing shame is difficult and isn't something that can be done quickly. We'll develop steps for healing abuse later in the book. But since shame is so complex and destructive, we want to get you started with some principles for healing toxic shame. These are things you can start doing now that will result in your feelings of shame decreasing over time. These tools are ones you can use throughout your life.

## ANCHOR TO GOD'S TRUTH

Satan loves to use shame to convince you that you're worthless, permanently defective, and unforgiveable. He also tries to convince you that God is as disgusted with you as you are with yourself, that God says the same things about you that others, including your abuser(s), have said. If Satan can keep you from turning to God, then he can keep you defeated by these destructive feelings. The following are some examples of the lies that people can believe about themselves and God when they're stuck in the grips of toxic shame. These are particularly common for those who have experienced abuse.

### Common shame-based lies:
- When God thinks about me, he gets sick to his stomach.
- God doesn't care about me.
- God doesn't pay attention to the details of my life.
- God could never forgive me for what I've done.
- God is angry; and if I go to him, he'll punish me.
- My body, especially my sexuality, is disgusting and dirty.
- God must not care about me if he didn't stop my abuse.
- God could never love me after all the bad things I've done.
- All my problems are proof that God is punishing me.

These lies *feel* very real and can cause you to stop in your tracks and not engage with God at all. Therefore, you need to anchor yourself in the truth about what God really thinks and feels about you. Otherwise, like a boat caught in a storm, you'll get pulled off course and risk being capsized.

One example of the truth about what God feels about you is found in Psalm 139. King David, the man who writes this Psalm, was guilty of multiple offenses that were severe enough to be given capital punishment! Even though David was married, he had sex with another man's wife named Bathsheba. Because he had supreme power and authority as the king, when he initiated having sex with Bathsheba, she was in a situation where she could have been killed if she refused. Therefore, it was essentially rape. After David got her pregnant, he tried to cover it up by having her husband and some of his friends murdered. David could certainly relate to feeling as if God wouldn't love or forgive him. Thankfully, when the prophet Nathan confronted David regarding his sexual sin and murder, David truly repented and experienced God's forgiveness. Listen to what David declared about himself and God:

GOD, investigate my life; get all the facts firsthand.
I'm an open book to you;
even from a distance, you know what I'm thinking.

You know when I leave and when I get back;
I'm never out of your sight.
You know everything I'm going to say
before I start the first sentence.
I look behind me and you're there,
then up ahead and you're there, too –
your reassuring presence, coming and going.
This is too much, too wonderful–
I can't take it all in!

Is there anyplace I can go to avoid your Spirit?
to be out of your sight?
If I climb to the sky, you're there!
If I go underground, you're there! ...

Oh yes, you shaped me first inside, then out;
you formed me in my mother's womb.
I thank you, High God—you're breathtaking!
Body and soul, I am marvelously made!
I worship in adoration—what a creation!
You know me inside and out,
you know every bone in my body;
You know exactly how I was made, bit by bit,
how I was sculpted from nothing into something.
Like an open book, you watched me grow from conception to birth;
all the stages of my life were spread out before you,
The days of my life all prepared
before I'd even lived one day.

Your thoughts—how rare, how beautiful!
God, I'll never comprehend them!
I couldn't even begin to count them –
any more than I could count the sand of the sea.
(Psalm 139:1–9, 13–18 *The Message*)

The LORD is compassionate and gracious,
slow to anger, abounding in love.
He will not always accuse,
nor will he harbor his anger forever;
he does not treat us as our sins deserve
or repay us according to our iniquities.
For as high as the heavens are above the earth,
so great is his love for those who fear him;
as far as the east is from the west,
so far has he removed our transgressions from us. (Psalm 103:8–12)

We encourage you to write these truths on a note card to keep in front of you as you walk through the "storm" of emotions you'll experience through the rest of this process. God loves you, shaped you while you were still in your mother's womb, knows what you need, and delights in forgiving and blessing you.

## FACE THE PAST

It's helpful to write out the incidents you feel guilty or shameful about. This list needs to include mistakes you've made, ways you've gotten in trouble, and also the ways you've been hurt. At this point it doesn't matter if it was guilt or shame, just write it down. Next, we'll sort it out. For now, just be totally honest about what you've done and what has been done to you.

## CLARIFY OWNERSHIP

After you've written out all the things that cause you to feel guilt or shame, you're going to need help to sort out what's what. There will be things you've done wrong that make you feel guilty, and then there will be the things that were done to you that cause you to feel shame.

The sins you've committed are your responsibility; they cause you to feel guilty—because you are. You'll need to confess to God, apologize to the people you've hurt, and learn to accept God's forgiveness. (We'll talk more about forgiveness in chapter eleven.) Once you've made those sins right with God and others, God will completely forgive you and set you free.

However, Satan will try to trick you into continuing to feel shame over sins that have been cleansed by God. The purpose of guilt is to motivate you to change your behavior. If you've made real changes and still feel horrible, that's shame and it is harmful.

The sins that others committed against you aren't your responsibility and are causing you to feel toxic shame. You don't need to feel guilt over wrong things others did to you. That's not your guilt—it's theirs. Begin to pray for God to help you see things as they really are. Own what's yours and let go of what's not.

## FRIENDS ARE A MUST

It's impossible to separate guilt from toxic shame alone. If you feel scared watching a 3-D movie, you need someone who's not wearing the glasses to remind you of what's real. Shame can make you want to isolate yourself and hide from other people, but we encourage you to do the opposite and include someone in this process. Remember, it's important to choose someone safe to share this type of personal information with. It's probably not a good idea just to start disclosing your pain to your partner in math class. In chapter nine we're going to talk about how to find a safe person and how to start trusting. When you've been hurt deeply by others, many times your "truster" is broken and you might give your heart away to those who do not know how to treasure and keep that information safe. Eventually you'll need others, though it may take a while for you to be ready for close relationships.

## HE WHO WALKS WITH THE WISE GROWS WISE, BUT A COMPANION OF FOOLS SUFFERS HARM. (PROVERBS 13:20)

One of the greatest challenges for survivors of abuse is to deal with the destructive shame that fills them like a giant cloud. But unlike physical clouds, shame doesn't just evaporate with time. It helps to face your guilt and toxic shame within a safe group of people who can help you see yourself for who you really are. The only remedy for toxic shame is being completely honest with God about yourself (the good, the bad, and the ugly) and finding that you're loved and accepted no matter what. When you experience that kind of love, it fights the shame-based lies that you're defective and unworthy of love from other people and even from God. It allows you to embrace the truth.

> I sought the LORD, and he answered me;
> he delivered me from all my fears.
> Those who look to him are radiant;
> their faces are never covered with shame.
> This poor man called, and the LORD heard him;
> he saved him out of all his troubles.
> The angel of the LORD encamps around those who fear him,
> and he delivers them. (Psalm 34:4–7)

# Chapter Seven Activities

## LEVEL ONE

Which stories could you relate to in this chapter? Write down what each story made you think about:

Guilt keeps us "in the fish bowl":

The "3-D lenses" of toxic shame:

Jessica's story and the shame cycle:

What Scripture in this chapter was most encouraging to you?

Think of some times you felt guilty for doing something wrong. Take some time to write about one situation where guilt motivated you to change your behavior but did not make you feel like you were a loser.

## LEVEL TWO

Is there anything in your life you've never told anyone? Write down those things in a place where you know that no one will read them, or you can rip up the paper after writing it.

Write in the space below what makes it scary to talk with someone about the things you wrote for the previous question.

How would it benefit you to tell someone the whole truth about what you've done and what has been done to you? Write about what it would take to make you feel that you could tell someone the truth about who you are and what you've done.

## LEVEL THREE

If you haven't done so already, write about all the things that have caused you to feel guilt or shame (or both). At first this is a messy process that requires lots of writing and reflection. Eventually, you'll begin to see what's what and distinguish between shame and guilt. For example:

Incident: I feel dirty and disgusting (and that I'm doing something wrong) anytime I feel attracted to someone. I guess I also feel bad because I know I shouldn't be hooking up at parties with guys I barely know. I can never tell anyone about that because if they knew what I was doing, they'd know how perverted I really am!

Shame: Feeling bad when I'm attracted to guys is shame. I felt the same way when I was being sexually abused by my uncle. I'm not dirty or disgusting. It's normal and healthy to feel sexual feelings. My uncle stole my innocence. It's okay to tell safe people what happened to me because it's his guilt, not mine! I didn't do anything wrong, and shame makes me want to hide.

Guilt: Having sex with guys I barely know is wrong, so it's healthy to feel guilty. That feeling is my conscience trying to protect me from getting hurt. I should listen to that feeling and get help to stop. It's okay to tell safe people that I'm struggling with this so I can understand why I'm doing it and get help.

Take some time to picture your abuser sitting in a chair across from you. Picture yourself handing back the shame that isn't yours. Is there a picture or an object that could represent the shame that you're handing back? What would you say to this person if you could?

What truth or Scripture from this chapter can you remember that will help you to not take back the shame that isn't yours? Write this Scripture on a small card and keep it where you'll see it every day.

# TRAUMA REACTIONS

Dear Anyone who finds this,
    I'm going to tell you about a kid named Jaime, he ended up killing himself because he couldn't handle his life. I'll start from the beginning, when he was five years old his father beat him so bad that his grandparents had to pull his father off him. When Jaime was seven years old he was molested by his uncle and that didn't stop until he was ten years old. At twelve he slit his wrists because all the girls he asked out told him he was ugly and made fun of him. At sixteen he still couldn't get any girls to go out with him because they always wanted to be friends. He stopped caring about everything after that. A year later he killed himself. You want to know how I know all this? Because I'm Jaime and I'm writing this letter before I die

                        — Jaime

A sophomore guy who had experienced physical and sexual abuse as a child wrote this letter. As you've seen throughout this book, abuse causes tremendous damage to a person's soul. Jaime experienced shame because he tried to hide his past from those who loved and wanted to help him. Because he kept those details of his life hidden, they couldn't heal and began spinning him into other effects of abuse that we'll discuss in this chapter.

Jaime's letter also illustrates the powerlessness he felt in his life. He described childhood abuse that he was powerless to stop. Then he went on to say that he still felt powerless because girls didn't like him and thought he was ugly. The only thing he could think of to take control would be to end his life. He couldn't change anything else in his life, but he was in control of whether he lived or died. No one could take that away from him.

Abuse causes feelings of powerlessness every time—no question. Psychologist Dan Allender notes that abused children are powerless to change their abusive family, stop the abuse, or take away the pain inside of them. "Abuse is extremely traumatic to the soul. It steals our security and normalcy, it extinguishes our hopes and dreams, destroys our wholeness, trust and self-esteem."[1]

## Trauma

Several years ago I (Kristi) was in a car accident. It was a small one, and it was my fault. I was on my cell phone (I know . . . that's bad, I don't do it anymore!), and I pulled into a fast-moving lane. I was distracted, so I didn't realize that a car was coming as fast as it was, and it hit me. I don't know if you've ever been in a car accident, but a strange thing happens: everything goes into slow motion and seems a little bit surreal. When that car hit me, I went numb—I wasn't scared, angry, upset, or anything. I was just strangely calm. I was able to pull off the road, call the police, fill out the paperwork (yes, I got a ticket), exchange insurance information, etc. But when it was all over and I started to drive away, my hands began to shake, and suddenly I felt nervous, guilty, and even a bit angry. Basically, I experienced a very small trauma, and my body, mind, and emotions went on "automatic pilot." Earlier I was numb and disconnected, so I was able to get through the immediate crisis relatively easily.

That's how God created and designed our bodies. When we experience any sort of trauma or extreme stress, we go into what's called "fight or flight" mode in order to get through it. That means that our bodies are prepared to either fight their way out of a situation, or flee (get out of there). Our breathing and heart rate increase, our muscles get tense, etc. My trauma was very small, and I was only in fight or flight mode for an hour, so I quickly returned to normal. But think of people who are raped, witness a shooting, are kidnapped, go to war, or are victims of a natural disaster. They might be in that mode for hours, days, weeks, or months.

Sometimes when the trauma ends, instead of returning to normal a person's body gets stuck in that fight or flight, automatic pilot mode. That's where problems like Post-Traumatic Stress Disorder come into play. That obviously happens to war veterans, but it also results from other traumas, including experiencing or witnessing abuse.

Even when a person is no longer in danger, the memory and emotions connected to the trauma can take on a life of their own. It's not uncommon for a survivor to have intense emotions triggered long after the event is over. This can happen through any of our senses: touch, taste, smell, vision, or hearing—and the person may have no idea what caused them to be triggered. The brain tells the body that it's in danger, so the body tenses up and responds. For example, we see this in the Hurricane Katrina survivor who feels terrified every time she takes a shower because that's where she was hiding when the hurricane hit her house, or the war veteran who hits the ground when he hears a car backfire, or the abuse survivor who jumps in fear when she is touched on the back.

The most powerful trigger can be the sense of smell.

I (Kristi) worked with a teenage sexual abuse survivor who was having panic attacks and didn't understand why. She'd been safe from her abuser (a family member) for a long time, had been in counseling, and knew logically that she wasn't in danger. The more we discussed the timing of her panic attacks, the more we realized that it happened mostly in the spring. As we talked, she remembered that her abuse also typically happened in the spring when this relative would come to visit from out of town. In Phoenix during the spring, a common scent is the smell of orange blossoms. That was the scent that was triggering my student. She realized that outside her bedroom window there was an orange tree. In the spring they would keep the windows in the house open and when this relative snuck into her room at night to abuse her, she could smell the orange blossoms from the tree outside her window. Now, just the smell of orange blossoms would send her body into a fight or flight response, even though she was currently safe from danger.

We're going to take a look at the three primary effects of trauma. Again, these are normal reactions to trauma and are God's design for our bodies, minds, and emotions to help us survive a dangerous event. But these reactions become a problem when they continue long after the trauma has ended. If you're experiencing these, you're not going crazy. It just means that you need some help working through the trauma.

# Trauma Effects

## HYPERAROUSAL

*Hyperarousal* is a condition in which the central nervous system of the body is "hyped up" long after the traumatic event has ended. Often when we hear the word *arousal*, we think of sexual feelings and reactions. The definition of *arousal* is "to stimulate to action or to physiological readiness for activity." *Sexual* arousal is just one way that term can be used. It can also be used when other, nonsexual parts of our body are getting ready for activity. So when your body is in fight or flight mode, your central nervous system is in high gear, as seen by increased heart rate, muscle contractions, and anxiety. That's the kind of hyperarousal we're talking about here.

I TREMBLED INSIDE WHEN I HEARD THIS;
MY LIPS QUIVERED WITH FEAR.
MY LEGS GAVE WAY BENEATH ME,
AND I SHOOK IN TERROR.
I WILL WAIT QUIETLY FOR THE COMING DAY
WHEN DISASTER WILL STRIKE THE PEOPLE WHO INVADE US.
(HABAKKUK 3:16 NLT)

It's important to recognize that the effects of chronic or severe trauma don't always just disappear with time. Time doesn't, in itself, heal all wounds. Abuse wounds can affect us in ways that greatly increase the chances of us being abused or taken advantage of again.

We (Steve and Celestia) can illustrate this with an incident that happened when Celestia was in Africa visiting our daughter Abby. Abby lives in the slums of Kampala, Uganda, and ministers full-time to street children. These are boys who've been abandoned by their families or who ran away from home, often because of severe abuse. On the streets they experience horrible physical and sexual abuse on a daily basis. To care for these boys, Abby and her team run two residential homes. For the boys still on the streets, they have programs several afternoons a week to feed and clothe them, offer basic medical care, education, and spiritual training.

Celestia was helping at one of their afternoon clinics, loving on the boys and giving out toothbrushes, when all of a sudden she was almost knocked flat by a blow to the back of her neck. She'd been hit by a rock the size of a tennis ball. A small boy, approximately five years old, had picked up the largest rock that would fit in his tiny hand and heaved it with all his might at Celestia. Before she even realized what had happened, Celestia heard a skirmish behind her and saw a cloud of dust as a mob of boys tackled this child and beat him severely. They were incensed that he had hurt their *jaja* (grandmother), Celestia. One by one the boys came to her, said they were sorry she had been stoned, and said, "It has been taken care of."

Why did this child stone the very workers who were loving him? Apparently, he wanted a toothbrush and the relief worker couldn't find the one he wanted. So he went into a blind rage, lashing out like a wild animal trying to protect himself from dangerous enemies. The cumulative effects of his trauma had triggered a rage response, which caused him to lash out and hurt someone, which in turn resulted in him experiencing more abuse. It also resulted in more shame, for once he came back to his senses he realized he had stoned one of the only people in his world who loved and cared for him.

While Steve and Celestia's story may seem to be an extreme example, this dynamic also plays out every day on school campuses.

I (Kristi) lead anger management groups that students are required to attend when they've been in a fight at school. One thing I hear over and over again are statements like this, "I don't know what happened—I just lost it." Or "What she did to me wasn't that big of a deal, but I just couldn't stop hitting her." I believe that, for many students, this is hyperarousal at work. For students who have a history of abuse or domestic violence in their homes, when someone at school calls them a name or puts them down (perhaps in the same way their parent does or did), that becomes a trauma trigger. They do, in fact, lose it. Many students ultimately don't have an anger management problem; they have a trauma problem.

## INTRUSION

The second reaction to trauma is called *intrusion*. Intrusion happens when a person vividly remembers traumatic events in flashbacks while awake, or nightmares while asleep.

A burglar who breaks into a house is called an "intruder," and these flashbacks and nightmares have virtually the same effect. They come to a person uninvited, invading his or her brain. A person experiencing this trauma reaction feels very nervous and insecure because he or she doesn't know when or where these thoughts and images are going to pop up. Many times the thoughts don't seem connected to the original trauma, which makes it all the more confusing. Here's an example:

Aaron was a freshman who came to see me (Kristi) because he was having nightmares. In the nightmare he was at the mall with his sister, when suddenly there was a robbery and his sister was taken hostage and killed. He explained feeling helpless as he tried to save her, but couldn't. Aaron had this nightmare over and over and was afraid to go to sleep. He was exhausted. Aaron was also terrified that something was going to happen to his sister in real life. When we talked about his life history, he revealed a major trauma. When Aaron was a small child, his mother's boyfriend would beat his mom in front of him.

When he was twelve years old, he decided to try and put a stop to this. His mother's boyfriend responded by laughing at him. He told Aaron that Aaron was weak and couldn't do anything to stop him, and then he pushed Aaron outside, locking the door behind him. He then proceeded to go back to beating Aaron's mother inside the house. Aaron's dream about his sister was different, but it had the same theme of powerlessness and fear over losing a woman whom he loved and desired to protect. In order to stop the dreams, Aaron would need to deal with the fear, pain, and powerlessness he experienced in the traumatic event involving his mom and her boyfriend.

WHEN I WAS IN DEEP TROUBLE,
I SEARCHED FOR THE LORD.
ALL NIGHT LONG I PRAYED, WITH HANDS LIFTED TOWARD HEAVEN,
BUT MY SOUL WAS NOT COMFORTED.
I THINK OF GOD, AND I MOAN,
OVERWHELMED WITH LONGING FOR HIS HELP.
(PSALM 77:2–3 NLT)

## NUMBING

The third effect of trauma is *numbing*, which is the emotional condition that involves the shutting down of all feelings so that, instead of feeling pain, one simply feels nothing. The person, consciously or unconsciously, decides it would be better to feel nothing at all than to risk feeling pain. If the abuse happens to an older child or teen, the person can sometimes remember shutting down his or her feelings. If the abuse happens to a young child, the person probably won't remember going numb because it's all he or she has ever known. In some cases, abuse survivors explain that during the abuse it felt as if they "left their bodies" and were somewhere in the room. In other instances, the numbing can take place long after the original trauma. If numbing doesn't work, then some people will use drugs or alcohol to feel completely numb.

DO NOT GAZE AT WINE WHEN IT IS RED,
WHEN IT SPARKLES IN THE CUP,
WHEN IT GOES DOWN SMOOTHLY!

> "THEY HIT ME," YOU WILL SAY, "BUT I'M NOT HURT!
> THEY BEAT ME, BUT I DON'T FEEL IT!
> WHEN WILL I WAKE UP
> SO I CAN FIND ANOTHER DRINK?" (PROVERBS 23:31, 35)

## Powerlessness

This chapter began with Jaime's suicide letter. He described his dark feelings of shame and powerlessness, which stemmed from the abuse he endured as a child. Jaime eventually decided that the only way he could change his painful life was to end it. We are thankful that most abuse survivors don't try to kill themselves. But most do experience another kind of death—death to hope. They come to believe that they can't change themselves, the abuse, or their world. Abuse survivors give up and just accept their painful lives and relationships even when there's clear evidence in front of them that they could break free.

> HOPE DEFERRED MAKES THE HEART SICK,
> BUT A LONGING FULFILLED IS A TREE OF LIFE. (PROVERBS 13:12)

On June 5, 2002, fourteen-year-old Elizabeth Smart was abducted from her bedroom at knifepoint by a drifter who thought he was God's prophet. Nine months later she was found alive less than twenty miles from her home. When a concerned citizen noticed Elizabeth walking through the streets with her captors, she was immediately recognized due to the flurry of media attention that surrounded her case. When police found her and asked her directly if she was Elizabeth Smart, she denied it and refused to acknowledge her need for help. How could Elizabeth, who had endured such tremendous abuse, not jump at the chance to be rescued? It was later discovered that during her nine months of captivity she was the victim of systematic brainwashing and ongoing sexual abuse. Ironically, it was *because* of her abuse that she couldn't ask for help. Elizabeth was experiencing the powerlessness that results from abuse.

### A LIFE STUCK IN TRAUMA

> "I [JESUS] CAME SO THEY CAN HAVE REAL AND ETERNAL LIFE,
> MORE AND BETTER LIFE THAN THEY EVER DREAMED OF."
> (JOHN 10:10 *THE MESSAGE*)

The tragedy of living a life stuck in trauma is that you continue to feel powerless over your present circumstances and, emotionally, you're too deadened to enjoy life. That is the exact *opposite* of how God meant your life to be. You were created for life—to experience it fully, to have joy and delight, to be able to trust others and God, and to have your needs met. *Living* life means *feeling* life.

I (Kristi) will never forget some advice my grandpa gave me a few years ago. He explained to me what he called "the secret of life." That had to be good, right? Well...you'll see. He went on to say, "The trick is not to get too excited about anything in life. That way if what you're excited about doesn't happen, you won't get too hurt or disappointed." I can see his logic—stay in the middle at all times. Don't feel happy, and then you won't feel sad either. My goal had always been to avoid painful feelings at all costs. I've realized in the past couple of years that by avoiding the painful feelings, I've been missing out on all the good ones, too.

> SO THE WOMEN HURRIED AWAY FROM THE TOMB, AFRAID YET FILLED WITH JOY, AND RAN TO TELL [JESUS'] DISCIPLES. (MATTHEW 28:8)

There's a great movie called *Garden State*.[2] It's about a guy named Andrew who had been numb to his emotions since a traumatic event when he was eight years old. When he was in his twenties, his mother died. Andrew then began to realize how numb he felt—he was experiencing the long-term effects of trauma.

> I haven't cried since I was a little kid. I didn't cry at my mom's funeral. I tried, you know? I thought of all the saddest things I could think of.... I just focused in on it. But nothing came. That actually made me sadder than anything...the fact that I just felt so numb.
>
> – "Andrew" in the movie *Garden State*

Later in the movie, Andrew decided that he didn't want to live his life like that anymore. He said, "I have felt so...numb to everything I have experienced in my life. Okay? ...What I want more than anything in the world is for it to be okay...for me to feel something again, even if it's pain." Then he said, "This is my life...this is it. I spent twenty-six years waiting for something else to start, so I don't think it's too much to take on, because it's everything there is. I see now it's all of it."

As Andrew comes alive emotionally, he experiences love, safety, and connection with others like he had never experienced. It was worth the pain to feel alive again. If you're numb, we encourage you to choose to be willing to feel again. It won't happen right away, but it must start with a willingness to face your feelings and the truth about your past. Over time you'll start to feel the bad—and you'll feel some really good things, too. That's what God created us for: life.

## A Mom's Love Letter

At the beginning of this chapter, you read a letter written by a student named Jaime who felt so much pain and powerlessness that he considered ending his own life. Luckily Jaime did not end his life. His letter was found by a teacher and then given to a counselor—and Jaime was able to express his pain and find the help and support he needed. Sadly, there are other students who act on their feelings of powerlessness and end their lives before they realize that their pain, while intense, can be healed.

LORD, YOU KNOW THE HOPES OF THE HELPLESS.
SURELY YOU WILL HEAR THEIR CRIES AND COMFORT THEM.
YOU WILL BRING JUSTICE TO THE ORPHANS AND THE OPPRESSED,
SO MERE PEOPLE CAN NO LONGER TERRIFY THEM.
I TRUST IN THE LORD FOR PROTECTION.
SO WHY DO YOU SAY TO ME,
"FLY LIKE A BIRD TO THE MOUNTAINS FOR SAFETY!"
(PSALM 10:17–11:1 NLT)

The following letter was written by a woman whose son committed suicide one month before his seventeenth birthday. Even though her son died more than twenty years ago, she still feels pain and misses him daily. It's our desire that her words will encourage you. We want you to read this as if it were written to you by someone in your life. We hope you can feel her love in your heart.

My dearest, most precious John,

I miss you. I long to hear your voice and to share days, hours, or even minutes with you. The love I have for you is still in my heart, and I am unable to express it to any other human being. It is yours alone. When you were born, your dad was so happy that he had a son! He announced that he had a fishing buddy. You would carry on his name. I will always treasure the nights you and I spent together when you were a tiny baby. You brought joy from just being you. You were intelligent, handsome every day of your life, fun and funny, interested in learning. You were deep and complicated, challenging, caring, cautious and sometimes fearful. Yet you were brave and independent.

Little did I know how unprepared I was to raise you children, and I know I made mistakes that hurt you. I know that the anger and frustration I saw in you as a teenager was really the disappointment you felt over not having the close family you desired. All of that anger in you worried me. What you needed was our love, support, time, understanding, patience, and guidance. You needed us to tell you that God knows and loves you beyond any happening ever in life. He made you, understands you, and is committed to you—regardless of your struggles. Instead though, your dad and I lectured to try and get you to do what we wanted you to do. I want you to know how sorry I am that you missed out on the love and nurturing that you deserved.

My heart will ache always for what I was not able to give you. You were dealing with painful emotions and circumstances beyond what a teen should have to face. They were obviously consuming you and you felt powerless to fix it. I wish I could have explained to you that life is like a book…each chapter is different from the other. When you're young and troubled, it may seem like the chapter you are experiencing is the only one and that nothing will ever change. The truth is that one, three, five years down the road our relationships, circumstances, and events are all different. Of course, we always have stress in our lives, but you would have had more life experience, more answers of your own from which to draw, and more people in your life to help support you when you asked.

John, when you made the choice to end your own life, I blamed myself, but I will not accept that responsibility anymore. Even though I will forever feel bad about what you did, it was you who made the choice to kill yourself. There are so many other choices you could have made, and I know we could have gotten through it together. But I understand that on that day it was just too much. You took yourself away from everyone who loves you. Your decision brought deep and lasting pain to many, many people.

If you were here today, all of our lives would be more complete. We would still have problems to deal with, but we would face them together. I can't help but wonder who you would have grown up to be, who you would have married, and what the voices of your children would have sounded like calling me "Grandma." I will always wish that you would have talked to me and asked for my opinion on your leaving. I would have begged and pleaded with you to stay! You matter! I truly and fully love and miss you, and I want you to be here.

Mom

# Chapter Eight Activities

## LEVEL ONE

Reread the letter written by Jaime at the beginning of the chapter. Can you relate to his feelings of powerlessness?

What situations have caused you to feel powerless?

How did you feel reading the letter to John at the end of the chapter? What did you think about as you read it?

## LEVEL TWO

When you feel powerless, what do you do to make yourself feel powerful again?

Look at the list of trauma effects below. Place a check next to any that you have experienced in your life. Circle any you feel are currently affecting your life in a negative way. Write next to each one how you experience that effect.

Hyperarousal:

Nightmares:

Flashbacks:

Numb emotions:

**LEVEL THREE**

What does *safe* mean to you? Do you feel you have a safe person, group, or place in your life? What makes them feel safe? Describe the effect this person or place has on you.

Think about the abuse in your own life and, using the feeling chart in the Appendix, describe in the space below the feelings you have. How has the abuse impacted you? What did the abuse steal from you, or what would have been different if the abuse had never happened? What might be something positive that God wants you to take away from the abuse he is helping you to heal from?

How might you pass on to others some of the healing and hope you have experienced?

Do you believe that we were created for life and to experience joy? Do you trust that God's got your back? What would it be like to live a life feeling alive, joyful, and trusting?

## Chapter Nine

# ISOLATION

Kelly Clarkson recorded an incredible song called "Because of You."[1] One line sums up the song well, "because of you I find it hard to trust not only me but everyone around me." Kelly said this about the song:

> "Because of You"…[is] about my family. It is about growing up in a broken home….I've talked to lots of friends who have seen domestic violence in their homes….If you see those things as a child, you see a family member cheating or people not trusting each other or people not communicating with each other, that affects you. You end up afraid to trust people because you think you're going to get [hurt]…It made me feel like, why would I want to open up and trust someone? …I wrote [this song] when I was sixteen. I have learned a lot since then….I used to be the most closed off person. I didn't want to get hurt. I had been messed over by friends, and I had been through a lot with my family. I didn't pity myself, but I did put a wall up. I'm smarter now, but I have a good relationship with God, and that's gotten better over the years. I'm a very trusting person now….I'm not going to let people [mess] me over left and right, but at the same time I'm not going to close myself off. That's a big step for me.[2]

Abuse produces profound long-term problems with relationships. Research clearly shows that abuse survivors have a harder time experiencing satisfying relationships and have a much more difficult time establishing relational trust than those who have not been abused. Abuse survivors are also more likely to experience divorce or separation when they do enter into relationships. These effects aren't just found in adults. Children and teenagers who have been abused are more distrustful, isolated, and have friendships that are less intimate than their nonabused peers.

Since I was eight, I have always had two things that have bothered me the most. The first is that my parents work so hard that they barely even see me, often leaving me alone. The second has bothered me since I figured it out. This is to say that life is so cruel that I decided to isolate myself from others, often never feeling or masking my true feelings, often being a loner in the eyes of others. From childhood until now, this has been my struggle.

– Jose, age seventeen

One of the first things we talked about in this book was that as humans we were created for intimate relationships—relationships that are nurturing, protecting, and real. This is such a fundamental human need that babies who are given food, water, shelter, and clothing yet are denied touch and affection will sometimes fail to thrive and eventually die. Humans desire and need intimate relationships. Even though past abuse *will* have a negative effect on our relationships, it doesn't have to be that way forever. When you understand how abuse affects you, you can take steps to heal from the abuse and experience healthy, satisfying relationships.

## Why Does Abuse Lead to Isolation?

Abuse creates several problems that hurt relationships. In chapter seven we looked at one of the most destructive results of abuse: shame. Shame powerfully contributes to isolation because it makes you feel defective, worthless, and makes you want to hide from others.

In chapter eight we spent a great deal of time talking about how abuse can cause you to numb your emotions. And you learned that shutting down negative emotions to avoid pain also shuts out the positive emotions. To form intimate relationships, you must first be aware of your own feelings. If you can't feel, then you can't enter into deep relationships with others because your deepest self is locked away. In their song "Easier to Run," Linkin Park describes pain from the past that causes such deep shame, woundedness, and helplessness that it's easier to go numb than to deal with the emotions:

It's easier to run
Replacing this pain with something numb
It's so much easier to go
Than face all this pain here all alone.[3]

– Linkin Park (2003)

"THE YOUNGER SON GOT TOGETHER ALL HE HAD, SET OFF FOR A DISTANT COUNTRY AND THERE SQUANDERED HIS WEALTH IN WILD LIVING. AFTER HE HAD SPENT EVERYTHING, THERE WAS A SEVERE FAMINE IN THAT WHOLE COUNTRY, AND HE BEGAN TO BE IN NEED.... HE LONGED TO FILL HIS STOMACH WITH THE PODS THAT THE PIGS WERE EATING, BUT NO ONE GAVE HIM ANYTHING. WHEN HE CAME TO HIS SENSES, HE SAID, '...I WILL SET OUT AND GO BACK TO MY FATHER AND SAY TO HIM: FATHER, I HAVE SINNED AGAINST HEAVEN AND AGAINST YOU. I AM NO LONGER WORTHY TO BE CALLED YOUR SON; MAKE ME LIKE ONE OF YOUR HIRED SERVANTS.'" (LUKE 15:13-14, 16-19)

We all have some faulty beliefs about the world. For example, *bad things don't happen to good people; God will never let evil people harm me; if I pray, the abuse will stop;* or *most people are basically good inside.* Abuse abruptly shatters those misbeliefs, causing us to become confused and distrustful of people and the world in general. It makes us feel safer and more powerful if we avoid the vulnerability and risk that comes with trusting others.

As children, we have an intuitive sense that we're to depend on and trust our parents. When that trust is violated by our primary caregivers, it makes little sense to trust other people who *aren't* obligated to love and care for us. Trauma victims' mistrust often involves far more than mistrust of their abusers. In fact, abused children very often feel more anger and mistrust toward the nonabusive parent for not protecting them than they do toward the abusive parent.

## Why Does Isolation Ruin Relationships?

Relational intimacy is built on emotional connection and risk taking. After we're abused, we can't risk someone getting too close and hurting us again. The relationships most impacted are with our friends and family, our dating relationships, and our view of God.

### FAMILY AND FRIENDS

Children who grow up in abusive families are traumatized and shamed, are not consistently loved and nurtured, and don't learn how to resolve conflicts. Therefore, all relationships are weakened—inside and outside one's family. Girls who experience sexual abuse from their fathers often report intense conflict with their mothers and other siblings who resent the "special" attention their fathers give them. Boys who've been abused tend to push *out* their pain onto others, and they often physically fight with their siblings and peers. Girls, on the other hand, tend to push *in* their abuse damage, which often results in depression and further isolates and weakens relationships with family and friends.[4]

We'd like to now look at a powerful (and extreme) biblical example of the way unhealthy families undermine and even destroy relationships. Judges is a book in the Old Testament that talks about a very bad time for the nation of Israel. The book is called "Judges" because this was a time period before Israel had a king, so individual men and women were the leaders of the nation. Those people were called "judges." Think of them as a military general, president, and court judge all rolled into one. The Israelites were struggling with violating God's guidelines. This resulted in broken intimacy with God and each other. They were worshiping idols, engaging in a lot of sexual sin, and were abusing each other. There are numerous recorded examples of unhealthy, fragmented, and abusive families.

One of the judges at this time was a man named Jephthah. His life and his family show us that in an abusive family, the members turn on each other and shame, blame, and isolate the victim(s). Sometimes the isolation is so extreme that the victim is even thrown out of the family. We read:

> Jephthah the Gileadite was a mighty warrior. His father was Gilead; his mother was a prostitute. Gilead's wife also bore him sons, and when they were grown up, they drove Jephthah away. "You are not going to get any inheritance in our family," they said, "because you are the son of another woman." So Jephthah fled from his brothers and settled in the land of Tob, where a gang of scoundrels gathered around him and followed him. (Judges 11:1–3)

Unhealthy families are not always this extreme in their treatment of the abuse survivor, but they do find plenty of less dramatic ways to push the person away.

The harmful impact of abuse on our relationships is such an important point that it deserves a bit more explanation. (Stick with us here.) Children who experience abuse growing up often do not develop the qualities and skills needed for building healthy relationships –appropriate self-confidence, a sense of self-worth, the ability to identify and share strong feelings, the ability to work through conflict, etc. Compounding matters, abuse survivors develop various relationally harmful "coping strategies" to deal with the pain of their abuse. These can include being aloof and telling yourself that you don't need people, becoming aggressive and intimidating, constantly manipulating others, never being transparent or vulnerable, or by bailing out of relationships whenever they start to become more intimate or emotionally challenging.

Earlier, we mentioned Linkin Park's song "Easier to Run," which explains the way abuse causes you to develop self-protective habits that shatter your ability to be truly intimate with others. You end up "alone" even if you have people around you. Linkin Park describes a dark secret they've kept locked away from everyone. They tell of wounds so deep they can't be seen by others—wounds that create shame that makes them want to simply ignore their past. They sadly confess, "It's easier to run." In short, abuse survivors often run from themselves, their family, and their friends.

ALL WHO HATE ME WHISPER ABOUT ME, IMAGINING THE WORST.... EVEN MY BEST FRIEND, THE ONE I TRUSTED COMPLETELY, THE ONE WHO SHARED MY FOOD, HAS TURNED AGAINST ME. (PSALM 41:7, 9 NLT)

## DATING RELATIONSHIPS

The first step to successful dating relationships is to be able to have good friendships. If a person is unable to work out conflict and have emotional closeness with *friends*, doing so in a *dating* relationship becomes nearly impossible. Therefore, if relationships aren't good with family and friends, the same patterns of conflict will leak into dating as well.

Teenage abuse survivors report significantly more verbal and physical abuse toward and from their partners. Among teenage sexual abuse survivors, there tends to be earlier and more frequent sexual activity. To some abuse survivors, it feels powerful to seduce someone and have sexual power over him. This can be an unhealthy, subconscious way to try to regain the power and control that was taken away from you when you were abused. For others, growing up without healthy physical touch and affection from parents causes all touch to feel sexual. Regardless of the specific reasons, dating relationships can be difficult for abuse survivors.

## VIEW OF GOD

When you've experienced significant pain, it's normal to feel suspicious and distant from God. This looks different for different people. Some people conclude that God doesn't even exist. Others believe that God exists but can't be trusted, so they keep him at a distance. That makes a lot of sense because if you've been hurt by *adults* who have more power than you do, then God is going to look *really* scary because he's all-powerful.

It's especially difficult to trust God when he's often described as a "father," and many of us have not had good experiences with our earthly fathers. This can result in you either avoiding God because of fear or being super-religious and doing all the right things to try and keep God happy.

"EVEN TODAY MY COMPLAINT IS BITTER; HIS HAND IS HEAVY IN SPITE OF MY GROANING. IF ONLY I KNEW WHERE TO FIND HIM; IF ONLY I COULD GO TO HIS DWELLING!...BUT IF I GO TO THE EAST, HE IS NOT THERE; IF I GO TO THE WEST, I DO NOT FIND HIM. WHEN HE IS AT WORK IN THE NORTH, I DO NOT SEE HIM; WHEN HE TURNS TO THE SOUTH, I CATCH NO GLIMPSE OF HIM....HE CARRIES OUT HIS DECREE AGAINST ME, AND MANY SUCH PLANS HE STILL HAS IN STORE. THAT IS WHY I AM TERRIFIED BEFORE HIM; WHEN I THINK OF ALL THIS, I FEAR HIM. GOD HAS MADE MY HEART FAINT; THE ALMIGHTY HAS TERRIFIED ME." (JOB 23:2-3, 8-9, 14-16)

## Healing and Reconnecting

Abuse creates shame, trauma, and isolation, so it's hard to engage in healthy relationships. And since we all desire relationships, it's very difficult to shut down that need. But even if you've been *negatively hurt* by old painful relationships, you can also be *positively healed* by new healthy relationships. What's important is finding safe, healthy friends. That's no small challenge. If you grow up seeing unhealthy relationships, you're naturally drawn to unhealthy people, since that's what's familiar.

ONE WHO HAS UNRELIABLE FRIENDS SOON COMES TO RUIN, BUT THERE IS A FRIEND WHO STICKS CLOSER THAN A BROTHER. (PROVERBS 18:24)

### HOW DO YOU START TO TRUST?

In college, I (Kristi) remember praying for good friendships in my life. Specifically, I prayed that I'd find an older woman who could be a friend, mentor, and role model to me. But people I'd trusted had hurt me, and I was hesitant to trust again. Even though I tried to keep myself isolated from relationships, there was a longing in my soul that I couldn't ignore.

Slowly, as I began to heal, I started to hang out with people who were different than the friends I'd always known. These people could express their emotions and talk about the hard stuff in their lives, which made me want them as friends. I could feel myself being pulled toward healthy relationships. Over time I began to share myself with these friends, and my ability to trust grew.

> TWO ARE BETTER THAN ONE,
> BECAUSE THEY HAVE A GOOD RETURN FOR THEIR LABOR:
> IF EITHER OF THEM FALLS DOWN,
> ONE CAN HELP THE OTHER.
> BUT PITY ANYONE WHO FALLS
> AND HAS NO ONE TO HELP THEM UP!
> ALSO, IF TWO LIE DOWN TOGETHER, THEY WILL KEEP WARM.
> BUT HOW CAN ONE KEEP WARM ALONE?
> THOUGH ONE MAY BE OVERPOWERED,
> TWO CAN DEFEND THEMSELVES.
> A CORD OF THREE STRANDS IS NOT QUICKLY BROKEN.
> (ECCLESIASTES 4:9-12)

After a few years of these peer friendships, I met a woman who asked me if she could meet with me regularly and be a mentor to me! This amazing woman has done more for my healing than anyone else. She's the first person with whom I could be completely honest and not censor my thoughts or feelings. She makes me feel safe because I know she'll love and accept me no matter what I say or do. I feel completely free to be myself, which makes me feel very alive inside. It is because of her friendship and guidance in my life that I now have other safe relationships where I can completely trust. These relationships in my life are mending my soul in ways I never knew were possible.

Since learning to trust is so difficult, I want to tell you a little more about how that process worked in my life. Then I'm going to give you some tips to trust based on my own experiences. You may already be doing some of these—that's great. But take a look through them and see if any might be helpful to you.

The ability to trust and heal ultimately comes from God empowering us and guiding us to safe people. Even though I'd been praying for years, it was when God knew I was ready that he finally brought someone into my life. When I met this woman, I soon came to admire her—God made it clear that this was someone I could learn from. We began meeting regularly so she could disciple me. She gave me a Bible study to do during the week, and then we'd meet to discuss it. But it wasn't a typical Bible study. She taught me how to journal honestly—to be authentic with God about how I was feeling. That was hard for me because I had trouble knowing how I was feeling, and it was difficult to express my emotions to anyone.

We didn't hang out only when we had a scheduled meeting. She let me come over to her house and hang out with her and her family. We had meals together. We went shopping together. Her husband helped me fix my car when it broke. We "did life" together. In that time I was able to observe her character—who she was and how she acted in different settings with different people.

In the first six months we were meeting together, I began to share more and more about myself. Some things were hard to talk about, but I took the risk and it went well. Nothing I said seemed to shock her, and I never felt judged. She encouraged me to take my pain to God and express it.

We'd been meeting regularly for more than six months before I felt that God was putting it on my heart to share the entire truth about my past. I remember clear as day the moment God told me it was time to come clean. I felt God telling me, "You can tell her." So I began to argue with God.

Have you ever done that? I told God that there was no way I was telling anyone the entire truth about my past. So, I made a deal with God. I told him that I would tell her all my secrets if she brought it up first. There. That should do it. I figured I was safe. No one I had ever known had talked about the type of stuff I was dealing with. But that very evening she began to comfortably share some struggles from her past that were strikingly similar to my own. You could have knocked me over with a feather! I felt completely terrified, but I also had a great sense of peace and love. I realized that night that only God could have brought someone that safe into my life. God loved me so much that he had laid out a path for my healing. Then, after I had made the decision to be honest, it took almost a month for me to tell her everything. It was a process that unfolded in layers.

BROTHERS AND SISTERS, IF SOMEONE IS CAUGHT IN A SIN, YOU WHO LIVE BY THE SPIRIT SHOULD RESTORE THAT PERSON GENTLY. BUT WATCH YOURSELVES, OR YOU ALSO MAY BE TEMPTED. CARRY EACH OTHER'S BURDENS, AND IN THIS WAY YOU WILL FULFILL THE LAW OF CHRIST. (GALATIANS 6:1-2)

The process of confessing my sins and pain to another person was life-changing for me. To know there's someone in this world who knows everything I've ever done and loves me anyway is very freeing. When I couldn't feel God's love directly, I saw it in my friend's eyes. It was the grace I experienced from her that opened up my heart to hearing God's truth in my life. To this day no one can call me out on something better than she does. Because there's a foundation of love and trust, I'm much more open to hearing truth (that's sometimes painful to hear) from her. This has resulted in the growth, healing, and maturity I was longing for.

It's important that we trust God first and then trust the process of his healing in our lives. God knows who you can trust and who you can be fully honest with. We can't rush the process either—it takes as long as it takes. For me, it started with a prayer in college stemming from my desire for relationships and accountability. I had no idea that God wouldn't answer that prayer until three years later. When he did, he was there beside me all the way.

Here are some tips we've learned as we've walked the path from isolation to connection.

## TIPS TO TRUST:

IF ANY OF YOU LACKS WISDOM, YOU SHOULD ASK GOD, WHO GIVES GENEROUSLY TO ALL WITHOUT FINDING FAULT, AND IT WILL BE GIVEN TO YOU. (JAMES 1:5)

### Ask God

It's important to ask and trust God to guide you and give you what you need. Specifically, ask God to lead you to at least one safe, trustworthy friend with whom you can build an authentic friendship. Be honest with God about your relational fears, struggles, and need for a good friend. Then trust God's timing. Psalm 62:8 says, "Trust in him at all times, O people; pour out your hearts to him, for God is our refuge."

### Take It Slow

Don't tell your deepest secret to the first person you meet. Take time to get to know that person. Trust takes time. You need to learn to share honestly and vulnerably with *safe* people—you can't share at a deeply personal level with those who aren't trustworthy. Jesus practiced this in his relationships. Just because someone *acts* like they want to spend time with you doesn't mean that he or she is a safe person you can disclose your heart to. When Jesus was at the middle of his ministry on earth, many people began to see all the cool things he was doing and wanted to follow him to have a relationship with him. John 2:23–25 says, "Many people noticed the signs he was displaying and…entrusted their lives to him. But Jesus didn't entrust his life to them. He knew them inside and out, [and] knew how untrustworthy they were. He didn't need any help in seeing right through them" (*The Message*).

You can also "take it slow" by taking small steps at the beginning. Think of it this way: You're not going to meet someone and let him borrow your car the first day. That would be insane. But you might let him borrow a pen during class. That's *still* a risk because he might not give it back. But if that happens, it will be okay because it's a tolerable loss—and you'll then know that person isn't trustworthy to borrow bigger things. If, over time, he's trustworthy with a pen, a hairbrush, a favorite CD, etc., then perhaps you can work up to letting him borrow a car.

Start small emotionally, too. Don't emotionally "give your car away" to someone you've just met. Start with a pen. Tell her about your day. Tell her something that has been frustrating you. Tell her about the guy in science class you think is cute. It's still a risk, but if she spreads a rumor, it will be more bearable if it's about something smaller than the pain you've experienced.

## Observe Character

Be aware that just because someone is a Christian doesn't automatically mean he or she has good character. Ask yourself if this person, over time, makes wise, discerning decisions. Obviously, we hope that other believers are the *first* ones who would have these character traits. But the reality is that Christians are broken too, and unless they've experienced God's grace and healing in their own lives, they don't yet know how to be safe people.

In the verse mentioned above, it says that Jesus could see right through the people who were trying to get close to him. He knew what no one had to tell him: certain people aren't trustworthy. But how can you discern a person's trustworthiness? You do that by observing their character over time in different circumstances. Look at their words and the way they treat other people when they don't think anyone is looking. Healthy people are consistent. If you notice a person is nice to some people and vicious to others, that's a red flag. A great example would be looking at how they treat someone who is unpopular at school. How do they talk about others when they're not around? Do they gossip about other people? Do they seem to enjoy getting up in people's business? Do they spread rumors? If so, that's not a safe person to share anything personal with.

TROUBLEMAKERS START FIGHTS;
GOSSIPS BREAK UP FRIENDSHIPS.
(PROVERBS 16:28 *THE MESSAGE*)

A safe person is able to ask you questions and be a good listener—it's not always about them. The following are three verses that point to some key character traits to help us identify safe, trustworthy, wise people. Proverbs 10:19–21 (NLT) says, "Too much talk leads to sin. Be sensible and keep your mouth shut. The words of the godly are like sterling silver; the heart of a fool is worthless. The words of the godly encourage many, but fools are destroyed by their lack of common sense." Proverbs 18:13 says, "He who answers before listening—that is his folly and his shame." Proverbs 20:5 says, "The purposes of a man's heart are deep waters, but a man of understanding draws them out."

## Determine Whether They Tell the Truth

Trust and relationships are built on truth and honesty. Watch out for sneaky people. If they are "good" liars and trick their parents, teachers, and friends easily, watch out because *you* could be next. Another way to tell if someone is truthful is to watch if they follow through on what they say. Someone who makes empty promises is not being truthful—and that's hurtful.

> KIND WORDS HEAL AND HELP;
> CUTTING WORDS WOUND AND MAIM.
> (PROVERBS 15:4 *THE MESSAGE*)

## Trust Your Instincts

This is a difficult statement to make because we've spent a lot of time in this book talking about how instincts get all out of whack when there's a history of abuse. God gave you an internal red flag system. You need to get back in tune with that—if your heart feels unsafe, don't ignore or override it. There's a difference between feeling like you're stretching yourself by taking a risk in a healthy relationship and pushing through the internal red flags triggered by an unsafe person. Listen closely and respond. Even though you won't "know an abuser when you see one," you *will* "know a safe person when you *feel* one."

## Take a Risk and Don't Give Up

Eventually it has to come to this: If you don't ever get out of your comfort zone and share something about your life with someone, you'll never know if that person's trustworthy. Relationships are always a risk—always. But it is a risk you need to take. Once God gives you someone you feel is safe, then we want to encourage you to begin sharing your story, including some of your struggles and sins.

Once you begin to take risks, keep going. The goal for your teen and young adult years is to make you into a healthy adult. In the process of

Isolation

growing up, a lot of things change. In middle school you feel like you need a large number of friends. As you go through high school, your number of friends will decrease and the emotional intimacy you have with your friends will increase. By the time you're in college and into your adult life, it's normal to have just a handful of very close friends. All that to say, don't give up if trust takes time to build.

**THEREFORE CONFESS YOUR SINS TO EACH OTHER AND PRAY FOR EACH OTHER SO THAT YOU MAY BE HEALED. THE PRAYER OF A RIGHTEOUS PERSON IS POWERFUL AND EFFECTIVE. (JAMES 5:16)**

### Get Grouped Up
Finally, some great places to find safe people are in a support group at school, a counseling group, church youth group, or college campus ministry. Those are typically places where hurting students go to find healing and to connect with friends and safe adults. That may be out of your comfort zone, but it could be the best risk you've ever taken!

**AND LET US CONSIDER HOW WE MAY SPUR ONE ANOTHER ON TOWARD LOVE AND GOOD DEEDS, NOT GIVING UP MEETING TOGETHER, AS SOME ARE IN THE HABIT OF DOING, BUT ENCOURAGING ONE ANOTHER—AND ALL THE MORE AS YOU SEE THE DAY APPROACHING. (HEBREWS 10:24-25)**

## Chapter Nine Activities

### LEVEL ONE
Reread the quote from Kelly Clarkson on page 129. Underline any line you can relate to. If you were to dedicate this song to someone who has hurt you, who would you dedicate it to?

Have you ever had a friend stab you in the back? How did that affect you? How does that affect your ability to trust someone?

If you decided to trust someone again, what's the worst thing that could happen?

**LEVEL TWO**
How has isolation hurt you in your relationships with your family, friends, or in dating?

How has the pain of abuse impacted your view of God?

What is one verse or truth you can claim from this chapter? Write it down on a card to remember and memorize.

Based on the tips for starting to trust, is there anyone in your life you'd like to try developing a deeper relationship with? What's one risk you can take this week in your relationship with that person?

## LEVEL THREE

The four dynamics that lead to isolation are shame, numb emotions, shattered beliefs about the world, and mistrust. Which ones have you experienced in your own life? Describe how or why each one leads you toward isolation.

On a separate piece of paper, journal your desire for the future. What areas do you want to be different in your life? How do you want to change your responses with respect to intimacy in your relationships? What do you long for relationally? What help/support do you need from God and others? Do you need to make any specific requests?

Look at this! We're ready to dive into the final section of the book. This is the exciting part. Now that we've looked at the profound soul damage created by abuse, we need to discover the process of healing and learn how to move forward. In the final three chapters, we'll map out a path to move into a future that holds emotional, spiritual, and relational healing. Sound good? Let's do it!

# PART FOUR
# Healing Your Pain

TAKE THE FIRST STEP IN FAITH.
YOU DON'T HAVE TO SEE THE
WHOLE STAIRCASE, JUST TAKE
THE FIRST STEP.

—MARTIN LUTHER KING JR.

Chapter Ten

# THE *MENDING THE SOUL* HEALING MODEL

The band Tenth Avenue North released a beautiful song in 2010 called "Healing Begins"[1] that truly captures the essence of what we're trying to convey to you through this book. We encourage you to check out this song and read all of its lyrics on your own because it talks about putting up walls so others think you're okay, being afraid to be real, feeling shame, and desiring healing. But probably the most poignant is the stanza: "This is where the healing begins…when you come to where you're broken within, the light meets the dark…." The writer of the song is correct. It's only when we face our pain and brokenness that God's grace can "collide with the dark inside of us." That's where God's healing work begins—at the very center of our brokenness.

The process of healing is just that—a process. We're going to talk about healing in terms of six stages that take a person from being disconnected to connected. When you've been deeply wounded, you need healing emotionally, relationally, and spiritually. We'll discuss all three areas in this section. We encourage you to do what you can as you're ready.

These stages to healing are not a simple checklist.[2] Most likely you'll move back and forth between them throughout the process, and everyone will move at a different pace. That's the beauty of it. Your *hurt* was unique to you, and your *healing* will be unique as well. These stages apply to you no matter what kind of pain you've experienced. Your pain could have been within the context of your family, dating, friendships, school, work, or church. The process is still the same. Let's describe each stage.

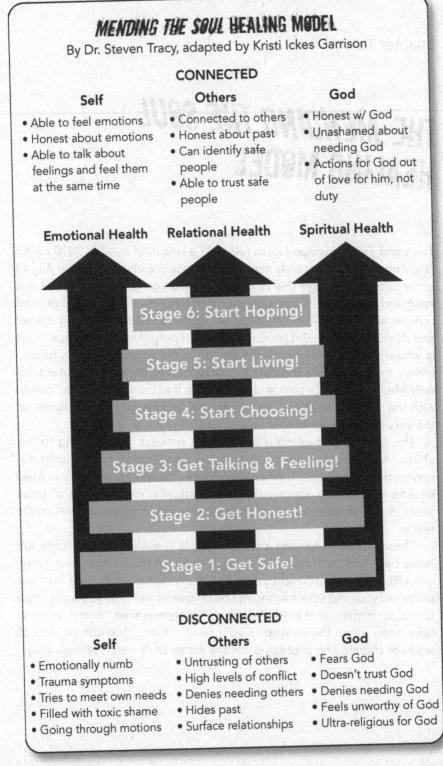

# MENDING THE SOUL HEALING MODEL

By Dr. Steven Tracy, adapted by Kristi Ickes Garrison

## CONNECTED

| Self | Others | God |
|---|---|---|
| • Able to feel emotions | • Connected to others | • Honest w/ God |
| • Honest about emotions | • Honest about past | • Unashamed about needing God |
| • Able to talk about feelings and feel them at the same time | • Can identify safe people | • Actions for God out of love for him, not duty |
| | • Able to trust safe people | |

**Emotional Health**    **Relational Health**    **Spiritual Health**

Stage 6: Start Hoping!

Stage 5: Start Living!

Stage 4: Start Choosing!

Stage 3: Get Talking & Feeling!

Stage 2: Get Honest!

Stage 1: Get Safe!

## DISCONNECTED

| Self | Others | God |
|---|---|---|
| • Emotionally numb | • Untrusting of others | • Fears God |
| • Trauma symptoms | • High levels of conflict | • Doesn't trust God |
| • Tries to meet own needs | • Denies needing others | • Denies needing God |
| • Filled with toxic shame | • Hides past | • Feels unworthy of God |
| • Going through motions | • Surface relationships | • Ultra-religious for God |

# Stage One: Get Safe!

It's very difficult for abuse victims to move into healthy relationships when their safety is still threatened. Therefore, the first step of healing is to find safety, both physical and emotional. If you're currently in a dangerous situation, it's important that you tell someone what's going on. If you're being physically hurt (in a way that leaves marks or bruises), if someone is touching you in a way that makes you uncomfortable, or if you feel threatened, then it's *essential* that you take the steps that are necessary to get safe.

Jesus models this example for us—he took necessary steps to establish safety from abusive people. John 11:53–54 says, "So from that day on [the religious leaders] plotted to take [Jesus'] life. Therefore Jesus no longer moved about publicly among the Jews. Instead he withdrew to a region near the desert, to a village called Ephraim, where he stayed with his disciples."

The fastest way to get safe is to talk to an adult and tell him or her what's happening to you. If you're under eighteen years of age and your abuse is physical or sexual, it's very likely that the adult will be required to consult the police or child protection agency in your area to figure out the best way to help you. *Sometimes* the result of that is the victim being removed from the home and placed with other family members or in a group home. More often, however, families are provided with counseling and then monitored closely to ensure the children's safety.

IN 2004, APPROXIMATELY 23 PERCENT OF ABUSED CHILDREN WERE PLACED IN FOSTER CARE, AND IT USUALLY WAS A SHORT-TERM PLACEMENT DURING THE COURSE OF THE INVESTIGATION. THAT MEANS 77 PERCENT OF CHILDREN WERE KEPT IN THEIR OWN HOMES, AND OTHER COUNSELING SERVICES WERE PUT IN PLACE TO HELP THE FAMILY.[3]

Obviously, this is a scary step because of the way shame can distort your sense of reality. You may feel that the abuse is your fault, or you may want to protect your parents and not get them in trouble. Perhaps you were intimidated into believing that if you told anyone you would be further harmed. We want to encourage you: Your abuse was out of your control, but now *you* are in control of whom you will tell and whether or not you begin the healing process. The choice is yours—only *you* know your situation and what you need to do in order to be safe.

If the abuse doesn't produce physical bruises, it's *less* likely that the police or a child protection agency will become involved, but it's still possible. Either way, you still need safety to heal. Talking to an adult will help you find a support group or counselor who can help you deal with your pain. It's essential that you find safe people to join you in this healing work.

## Stage Two: Get Honest!

Many times our biggest fear about being honest is that the pain will be so great we won't be able to stand it. The next stage in the healing process is to choose to stop protecting ourselves by denying and minimizing the truth about our abuse. Yes, there will be emotional pain involved, but since you survived the initial pain of the abuse, you'll survive this as well. The difference is that this time you'll have other people who love you to help you through it.

We've already spent some time looking at the results of abuse and talking about how a person can become quite skilled at numbing and avoiding pain. Since your emotions aren't a light switch that can be turned on and off, you can't just *start* feeling. It takes time. Stage Two involves a *deliberate choice* to no longer suppress the truth and a *willingness* to enter into whatever feelings surface as you stop denying what happened to you.

In your healing, God asks you to be willing to see your pain and abuse for what it really is. This may go against what your instincts tell you, because it's painful. In those painful times remember that your own strategies to protect yourself from the pain and to heal yourself aren't working. At some point you must trust God's healing process because you realize that he knows best.

> TRUST IN THE LORD WITH ALL YOUR HEART
> AND LEAN NOT ON YOUR OWN UNDERSTANDING....
> THIS WILL BRING HEALTH TO YOUR BODY
> AND NOURISHMENT TO YOUR BONES. (PROVERBS 3:5, 8)

A teenage boy drew the following picture. It describes his emotional and spiritual condition after being exposed to sexual abuse in a church, and it vividly illustrates both the tendency of abuse victims to lean on themselves for their healing and how that does not work. The picture is titled, "Weathered and Tired." Written on the boy's face and body are various phrases that articulate drastic reliance on self for healing and protection: "I have to hold back the darkness." "I must endure." "I have to be strong." "I have to withstand." "I cannot fail." Around the heart is written "Make the hurting stop!" Sadly, no matter how much energy he puts into this effort, he can't endure, he can't be strong enough, he can't hold back the darkness, and he can't heal his hurting heart on his own.[4]

Instead of settling for the temporary relief that comes from ignoring or numbing your feelings, make a choice to face the truth about your past and feel what you need to feel. That will eventually be what sets you free. It's time to get honest.

"THEN YOU WILL KNOW THE TRUTH, AND THE TRUTH WILL SET YOU FREE." (JOHN 8:32)

WHAT YOU'RE AFTER IS TRUTH FROM THE INSIDE OUT. ENTER ME, THEN; CONCEIVE A NEW, TRUE LIFE. (PSALM 51:6 *THE MESSAGE*)

## Stage Three: Get Talking and Feeling!

This stage tends to be the most difficult and time-consuming part of the healing process. In the exercises at the end of the chapter, we'll give you some activities and suggestion to help get you started. There are many reasons you may have shut down your ability to feel pain, and this can seem quite difficult—but don't give up on this one. Just start wherever you can. You can't force the feelings to come, but you *can* make a choice to start telling your story in safe, appropriate ways. You might start to journal and write down your story. You might take the risk to share your story with a close, trusted friend. Or perhaps you can share in a support group or even with a counselor, teacher, or pastor.

This stage tends to happen in layers. You might share your story once, twice, even a half-dozen times and not feel anything at all. The most difficult part of this process is *feeling* your story, but that's also the most important part. A common counselor saying (they must teach it in counselor school) is "You've got to feel to heal." Yeah, we know, cheesy—but it's really true. It's also easier said than done. It's sad when students recount horrible stories of abuse with little or even no emotion. It almost sounds as if they're reading a report they wrote for their history class.

TRUST IN HIM AT ALL TIMES, YOU PEOPLE;
POUR OUT YOUR HEARTS TO HIM,
FOR GOD IS OUR REFUGE. (PSALM 62:8)

It's okay to start there initially—to write your story without any emotions. Don't beat yourself up if it takes a while to feel. We can trust that when you're ready, God will eventually start to bring up the appropriate emotions. When these emotions come, it can be scary—especially if they've been shut off for a long time. Think of your journal as a vault where you can dump your feelings without anyone seeing them. You don't have to worry about hurting others when you write in your journal. Say what you wish you could say to the people who've hurt you. Yell, scream, do what you need to do. If this process begins to feel overwhelming, or if you don't feel better after dumping your feelings into your journal, then it's a very good idea to get the help of a professional counselor. We'll talk about how to get a counselor in the final chapter of this book (but feel free to skip ahead now, if you like).

O LORD, HOW LONG WILL YOU FORGET ME? FOREVER?
HOW LONG WILL YOU LOOK THE OTHER WAY?
HOW LONG MUST I STRUGGLE WITH ANGUISH IN MY SOUL,
WITH SORROW IN MY HEART EVERY DAY?
HOW LONG WILL MY ENEMY HAVE THE UPPER HAND?
TURN AND ANSWER ME, O LORD MY GOD!
RESTORE THE SPARKLE TO MY EYES, OR I WILL DIE.
(PSALM 13:1–3 NLT)

Be patient, take your time, and be gentle with yourself. This isn't a race. There's no prize for finishing first. When you're able to feel the pain, it will come. Then you'll shed the toxic shame created by the abuse, and you'll be able to move to the next stage—one that involves correcting the distortions caused by abuse.

## Stage Four: Start Choosing!

As seen in the chart on the next page, most people have come to believe numerous shame-based lies about themselves, others, and God. All such lies are very damaging. Once you're able to identify the lies created by your pain or abuse, then the challenge is making a *choice* to believe the truth, even when the lies *feel* right.

In the late '90s there was a segment on *Saturday Night Live* called "Daily Affirmation with Stuart Smalley." In order to feel good about himself, Stuart would end each segment by looking in the mirror and saying, "I'm good enough, I'm smart enough, and doggone it, people like me." That sounds great, but how does it make you feel better to just *decide* you're okay? What if you don't *feel* okay? How can you believe *yourself*?

You need someone greater or better than yourself to tell you that you're okay. You can believe you're okay because the loving Creator of the universe says so. It also helps to see yourself through the eyes of the people you admire. When people you respect accept you, it makes it easier for you to accept yourself. We don't know about you, but we would trust those methods more than Stuart Smalley or ourselves. The chart on the next page will tell you how it works.

| LIES | TRUTH |
|---|---|

### SELF

1. I could have done something to prevent my abuse. It was my fault.

2. My sexual urges are gross and show that I'm perverted.

3. I'm incapable of having healthy dating relationships. I'll only be used.

### SELF

1. I can reject toxic shame and give it back to my abuser. It was his/her fault, not mine.

2. My body is designed to experience sexual pleasure. My body is not bad.

3. I was created unique. There is no one like me. I should not settle for less than the best.

### OTHERS

1. I can't let anyone know the real me or they'll think I'm bad.

2. I can't trust anyone else; people will only hurt me.

3. All guys are jerks...they only want sex and to meet their own needs.

### OTHERS

1. All of us have issues and pain from our past. If I can accept me, then others can too.

2. I can learn to trust safe people who will love me and care for me.

3. Men are responsible to protect and cherish women. I can believe that good guys exist.

### GOD

1. What has God ever done for me if he didn't stop my abuse when I asked?

2. God could never love me after all the bad things I've done.

3. All of my problems are proof that God is punishing me.

### GOD

1. I can trust God to bring good out of evil. God is bigger than my abusers, will heal me, and will punish my abusers for what they did.

2. God loves me in spite of knowing everything about me, and God cares about all of my hidden struggles.

3. God loves me no matter what I've done and wants the best for my life.

The truths found in the chart all come directly from Scripture. Only God has the authority to speak truths into your life that are powerful enough to combat the painful lies caused by abuse. A lovely little book that illustrates this point is *Life of the Beloved* by Henri Nouwen. He says the following about using the truths found in God's Word when we feel unloved or unwanted:

> When we do not feel loved by those who gave us life, we often suffer our whole life-long from low self-esteem that can lead easily to depression, despair, and even suicide. In the midst of this extremely painful reality, we have to dare to reclaim the truth that we are God's chosen ones....Every time you feel hurt, offended, or rejected you have to dare to say to yourself: "These feelings, strong as they may be, are not telling me the truth about myself. The truth, even though I cannot feel it right now, is that I am the chosen child of God, precious in God's eyes, called the beloved from all eternity, and held safe in an everlasting embrace."[5]

Ultimately, God is the One who'll allow you to feel these truths. For now, you can, by faith, accept that it's true because God says so! Much of the Christian life is a battle against Satan's lies. We must choose to believe God's truth. Paul had to remind the Corinthians that Satan spreads lies and that a big part of living the Christian life is to discipline our mind by choosing to believe God's truth.

FOR THOUGH WE LIVE IN THE WORLD, WE DO NOT WAGE WAR AS THE WORLD DOES. THE WEAPONS WE FIGHT WITH ARE NOT THE WEAPONS OF THE WORLD. ON THE CONTRARY, THEY HAVE DIVINE POWER TO DEMOLISH STRONGHOLDS. WE DEMOLISH ARGUMENTS AND EVERY PRETENSION THAT SETS ITSELF UP AGAINST THE KNOWLEDGE OF GOD, AND WE TAKE CAPTIVE EVERY THOUGHT TO MAKE IT OBEDIENT TO CHRIST. (2 CORINTHIANS 10:3-5)

What's interesting is that many times the area in which a person struggles with the most shame ends up being one of the best parts of who they are.

For *years* I (Kristi) prided myself on being very unemotional. I thought showing emotion (especially sadness) was weak, and I felt very good about the fact that I rarely cried. However, since I've done my own healing

I've learned that I'm actually a *very* emotional person. I get really excited and passionate about things, I'm very expressive and engaging with people, and I also hurt very deeply at times. That's my *original* design, and it turns out that's also what makes me good at working with students. Generally, I'm told that my excitement, energy, and compassion are why students trust me and feel that they can relate to me. Wow! Who would have known that my emotions—the *very thing* that was intended in me for *good*—was something I felt was a weakness to be rejected. So it's time to start choosing. Choose to believe God's truth about who you really are and reject the lies that your abuse has created. It may not feel like the truth at first, but you can make a decision to believe that it is. You know why? Because you're good enough, you're smart enough, and doggone it...(just kidding)!

## Stage Five: Start Living!

You read in chapter eight that some reactions to trauma are automatic, unconscious choices—especially in the early stages after the abuse. You also read in chapter six that when needs are unmet, a person sometimes uses risky behavior to attempt to meet those needs. Even though risky behaviors and trauma reactions serve a purpose for a while, they eventually become the very things that hold you back. They keep you from understanding yourself and having healthy relationships with others. When you decide to manage the pain instead of reaching outside of yourself for help, you're unable to truly live—in your efforts to protect yourself from pain, you end up blocking yourself from life, joy, and intimacy with others.

In order to truly start living, you must decide to turn away from the things that have been "holding you together." As you start to tell your story and feel pain, you'll instantly be tempted to run from that pain. Maybe it will be drugs, alcohol, sex, avoiding feelings through denial, or distracting yourself through sports and getting good grades. It can be anything that allows you to avoid feeling and experiencing the truth about what's going on in your life.

As a survivor, you likely feel as if you need to deaden the pain. However, although those behaviors may feel like they are giving you life, in the end it's just a slow death. Jesus gives you the option of living another way: Instead of trying to control your life yourself, give up that control, let your emotions come, and reach out for support. Start living by choosing to give up the behaviors that deaden you. The path of life and healing doesn't work if you deny reality or deaden your emotions.

In Matthew 10:38–39 Jesus says, "Anyone who does not take his cross and follow me is not worthy of me. Whoever finds his life will lose it, and whoever loses his life for my sake will find it." This would have been a very shocking statement to the audience because the cross was an instrument of execution—a very final and very *real* death. Jesus was saying that his followers needed to be willing to die to themselves (meaning they needed to be willing to give up doing life on their own terms, by their own will, apart from God). What Jesus told them to do was the opposite of logic: he told them to stop protecting themselves and doing what *they* felt was best—instead they were to give the control to him.

## Stage Six: Start Hoping!

It's only after you've experienced the pain and sadness that come with looking at your past that you can truly have hope for your future. The sadness over the things that have happened in your past comes at all stages throughout the healing process. Starting to hope, however, happens toward the *end* of our healing, which is why it's our final stage in this model.

I WILL EXALT YOU, LORD,
FOR YOU LIFTED ME OUT OF THE DEPTHS
AND DID NOT LET MY ENEMIES GLOAT OVER ME.
LORD MY GOD, I CALLED YOU FOR HELP
AND YOU HEALED ME.
YOU LORD, BROUGHT ME UP FROM THE REALM OF THE DEAD;
YOU SPARED ME FROM GOING DOWN TO THE PIT....
"HEAR, LORD, AND BE MERCIFUL TO ME;
LORD, BE MY HELP."
YOU TURNED MY WAILING INTO DANCING;
YOU REMOVED MY SACKCLOTH AND CLOTHED ME WITH JOY,
THAT MY HEART MAY SING TO YOU AND NOT BE SILENT.
LORD MY GOD, I WILL PRAISE YOU FOREVER."
(PSALM 30:1-3, 10-12)

Sadness over (or mourning for) our losses is an honest response to what has actually happened, and this sadness is necessary for complete healing. Because abuse creates such deep wounds in so many areas of life, there are many losses survivors must recognize and mourn. For instance, survivors often need to mourn the loss of their innocence, their virginity, their parents' love, their childhood, their glowing image of their family, and intimacy with other family members.

Ultimately, God is your only secure source of this hope. Ironically, mourning the losses from past abuse allows you to meet God in the present and provides hope for the future. How wonderful to be able to confidently understand how pain from past abuse has impacted your life, then face your past and finally be free from its enslaving effects! It excites us to know that you can have a future full of hope and healthy relationships.

## Chapter Ten Activities

### LEVEL ONE

Look at the descriptions of *disconnected* versus *connected* in the healing model on page 148. Circle the descriptions on the healing model that best describe you right now. Does your level of connection change depending on the relationship? Why do you think that is?

Look at the description of the "connected" person on the healing model. Do you know anyone like that? Who is it? What do you admire about that person? How do you feel when you are with him or her?

Record the "truths" and any verses of Scripture that you need to remember. Copy them on 3x5 note cards and keep them with you throughout the day. Memorizing these truths will help you remember them when you need them most.

## LEVEL TWO

Look back at the healing model on page 148. Color the stages in the following way:

> **GREEN** (I'm willing to do this.)
>
> **YELLOW** (I feel cautious about this, but I'll give it a try.)
>
> **RED** (I do not want to do this—I'm not ready yet.)
>
> Healing starts with willingness. Don't worry about the red stages yet—just start with the green and go from there.

## LEVEL THREE

Here we're going to give you many suggestions for how you can work each stage. This is a lot of information, and we don't want you to feel overwhelmed. You'll need to get a journal or sheets of paper to complete these exercises—there's not enough room here. Remember, this isn't a checklist you have to go through in a particular order. Read through the list below and if you feel pulled to do an activity, then that's your sign to do it. It's okay to jump around in the stages until you've through worked every one. So feel free to just dive in!

### Stage One: Get Safe!

Do you feel physically safe from harm in your home? What are the risks and benefits of talking with an adult about your physical safety? How would you know when you need to involve others to make you safe?

Who could you talk to about your situation who can help you get safe? In the space below, write the names of three "safe" people and their phone numbers, in case you were to need them.

## Stage Two: Get Honest!

Are there any things that you've done or things that have happened to you that you've never told anyone about? Take some time to write those things down now. Writing is a first step to help you at least admit these things to yourself, which will be your foundation for later telling someone else. It also relieves you of some of the pain you've been carrying—even if it just goes into your journal. Writing is doing *something* about the situation

## Stage Three: Get Talking and Feeling!

If you've never done so, take some time to write out your life story on a separate piece of paper. You can use your timeline to make sure you don't miss any significant events, but actually write out the entire thing like a story. After you've written out your story, go back through and try to write down a feeling word with each event. If you read your story and don't feel any emotions, then write down how someone else might feel if he or she had experienced what you have written. Use the feeling chart in the Appendix if you have trouble coming up with anything. Begin thinking about the person who might be able to read your story. It might be someone in your small group or an adult you trust. When you're ready to share your story, take a risk and do so. Note: Even when you're ready, you'll still feel nervous and it *will* be a risk. Remember, if you wait until you're not nervous, then you'll never share.

## Stage Four: Start Choosing!

Look at the chart of truth and lies on page 154. Read through the list of lies on the left side and put a star next to any that you can relate to. Look at each truthful statement next to the lies that you chose. Write each of those statements on an index card and put them somewhere you'll see them regularly. As you share your story with safe people, they'll be able to help you spot other lies you're unknowingly believing. Then you can ask for help identifying your truths. You might also find it helpful to write encouraging quotes, notes from friends, or Bible verses on index cards so you can see them regularly. When you're done with them, you can tape them into your journal. In time, you'll be able to look back on your healing and see measurable growth!

## Stage Five: Start Living!

What are the behaviors—positive or negative—you use to protect yourself from pain? Identifying these behaviors is essential. Once you identify them, you'll be more likely to notice them when you use them. That will give you the opportunity to work at making the choice not to use them. Change happens in a process that all starts with awareness and practice:

A. You identify your coping behaviors after you've used them.
B. You notice the coping behaviors while you're using them.
C. You recognize the common situations that tempt you to use your coping behaviors ahead of time, and you choose to set them aside and use new, healthier strategies instead (like journaling or reaching out to God and others).
D. You use the new healthy strategies automatically, without having to think about it.

## Stage Six: Start Hoping!

Mourning your losses is being honest about what happened to you in your past and feeling the sadness about the ways you've missed out. In this chapter we discussed some examples. What are your reactions to that information? Are there any specific losses from your childhood you feel sad about? What gives you hope that your future will be different? Take some time to write about your thoughts and feelings.

# FORGIVENESS

## THE WEAK CAN NEVER FORGIVE; FORGIVENESS IS THE ATTRIBUTE OF THE STRONG.
## —MOHANDAS GANDHI

"Are you kidding me? I'm supposed to do *what*?"

Hold on! Before you chuck this book out the window of a moving car, hear us out. Forgiveness can sound cliché—like something people throw around to say that what happened to you is no big deal. *It is a big deal.* We're guessing you've figured that out since you've read this far. And we do need to discuss forgiveness, since our goal is for you to have spiritual, emotional, and relational health. First, we'll briefly discuss forgiving your-self and God; then we'll spend some time talking about what it looks like to forgive others.

## Experiencing Forgiveness

In chapter seven we talked about healthy and toxic shame and the pro-cess of overcoming that shame. That's what starts the process of self-forgiveness. You need to sort out what you feel guilty and/or shameful about. Then you need to clarify ownership—step up to take responsibility for what's your stuff and give away the stuff that belongs to the one who hurt you. You must refuse to accept shame over the things that were done *to* you. Remember that Satan is a master at confusing guilt and shame in your life. Often you will feel shame for the stuff that isn't yours, but then you won't feel guilt for the stuff that is yours to own, confess, and clean up.

After you let go of feeling responsible for what others have wrongly done to you, you need to receive God's forgiveness for the things you've done wrong. This is no easy task.

I (Kristi) felt like something was wrong with me, and I couldn't fix my emotional and behavioral problems on my own, so I got the help of a professional counselor. My counselor made me feel very safe and allowed me to say anything without being judged or put down. She taught me that we all do wrong things in order to deal with our pain. Those wrong things might look different for each person but we all do them.

## JESUS SAID, "IT IS NOT THE HEALTHY WHO NEED A DOCTOR, BUT THE SICK....FOR I HAVE NOT COME TO CALL THE RIGHTEOUS, BUT SINNERS." (MATTHEW 9:12-13)

I'll never forget a time when I was struggling to admit some of the shameful behaviors from my past that I had never told anyone about. Even though I knew that I couldn't be free until I got it off my chest, I sat in my counselor's office, trapped in my own toxic shame and self-hate, unable to talk.

She repeated over and over, "Your behavior measures how much you were hurt."

Finally, I was able to tell her the truth about my past, and I was amazed when she loved and accepted me.

She modeled for me how God views our sins. He loves us unconditionally and wants to forgive us. He sent his Son to die for our sins. But to experience his forgiveness, we must admit (confess) our sins to him and ask him for forgiveness. No sin is unforgiveable. First John 1:9 says, "If we confess our sins, he is faithful and just and will forgive us our sins and purify us from all unrighteousness." The only person God can't or won't forgive is the person who refuses to admit that he or she has sinned (1 John 1:10). Forgiving myself came only after I shared the truth with a safe person and refused to run from the shame I felt—then I saw myself through another person's compassionate eyes.

That night while driving home, I heard the final lyrics of Green Day's song "Jesus of Suburbia" in an entirely new light: I was finally able to let myself off the hook for the choices I'd made in my pain.

I don't feel any shame, I won't apologize
When there ain't nowhere you can go.
Running away from pain
When you've been victimized.[1]

– Green Day (2004)

That night I took the first steps in the process of experiencing God's forgiveness. I decided I wasn't going to punish myself anymore for past sins that God had forgiven. I shared the entire truth about my past with someone I trusted, and she helped me sort out my guilt and shame. I felt empowered to take responsibility for what I'd done wrong, and I felt compassion for myself regarding the things that had been done to me.

## Forgiving God

Forgiving God? That may sound funny, and perhaps it's an idea you've never before considered. If God is supposed to be perfect, then how can you forgive him? We know that your trust in God can be shattered when there's abuse in your past. It may feel as though God has abandoned you and can no longer be trusted. The process of forgiving God involves wrestling with him, sharing your frustrations, confusion, and even anger. It's in that place of honesty that you can ask him to meet you. Once you get honest with God, you can begin to learn who he really is. God *did not* cause your abuse, nor does he approve of it. He will deal very strongly with your abuser(s), and he will comfort you in your healing. He will also use your pain for good in the future—if you let him. We encourage you to continue to wrestle with God over your feelings toward him—ask him to make himself known to you and to make plain his plans for you, ask him to show you his purpose to heal your pain and use it for good. He loves it when you come to him in this way!

THE LORD EXAMINES THE RIGHTEOUS,
BUT THE WICKED THOSE WHO LOVE VIOLENCE
HE HATES WITH A PASSION.
ON THE WICKED HE WILL RAIN
FIERY COALS AND BURNING SULFUR;
A SCORCHING WIND WILL BE THEIR LOT.
FOR THE LORD IS RIGHTEOUS,
HE LOVES JUSTICE;
THE UPRIGHT WILL SEE HIS FACE. (PSALM 11:5-7)

The prophet Habakkuk complained to God and poured out his sorrow over the violence and pain he saw around him. God responded, but the response only raised more questions. This started a back-and-forth "discussion" between Habakkuk and God. Here's how it started out:

How long, O LORD, must I call for help,
but you do not listen?
Or cry out to you, "Violence!"

but you do not save?
Why do you make me look at injustice?
Why do you tolerate wrong?
Destruction and violence are before me;
there is strife, and conflict abounds.
Therefore the law is paralyzed,
and justice never prevails.
The wicked hem in the righteous,
so that justice is perverted (Habakkuk 1:2–4).

Ultimately, God met him in that place of frustration and doubt. Even though God didn't answer all his questions, at the end, God showed himself to Habakkuk. In 3:18–19 the prophet is able to say, "Yet I will rejoice in the LORD, I will be joyful in God my Savior. The Sovereign LORD is my strength; he makes my feet like the feet of a deer, he enables me to go on the heights." God may never answer all of your questions; but if you keep pursuing him, he will respond. In time, you'll look back and realize that some of your most intimate moments with the Lord came out of those times in which you wrestled with God and pled with him to speak to you.

# Forgiving Others

This is where we need to spend some time. You need to know that forgiveness is a controversial topic in counseling circles. Many counselors will start painting picket signs when they see that we wrote a chapter on forgiveness. That's because some people teach really harmful things about forgiveness. So before we tell you what forgiveness is, we need to share with you what it's not:

> After my dad got help, things started getting back to normal—but better than before. For some reason, though, as much as he acted like the abuse never happened, I couldn't. I've never been able to even till this day. I keep hatred toward him, and whenever he just raises his voice at me, I just get mad and can't stand him. I feel like he treated me so bad that he doesn't deserve for me to forgive him and give him another chance. That's why my struggle is letting go of the past, because I feel as though I can't and shouldn't.
>
> – Martin, age fourteen

## FORGIVENESS IS NOT—
### Saying the Abuse Was Okay
A common mistaken belief about forgiveness is that when you forgive, you're saying what the other person did wasn't a big deal. The truth is, you can forgive others and still communicate that what was done to you *is* a very big deal and was wrong.

## Letting the Person off the Hook

If a person has done something wrong, then that person deserves the consequences he or she gets. This might mean legal actions, a broken relationship, loss of custody of one's children, divorce, or loss of others' trust. Forgiving someone doesn't mean that you forget what they did to you, blindly trust them, and risk getting abused again.

## Letting Go of All Negative Emotions

When you're hurt you're going to have a variety of appropriate emotions such as fear, anger, suspicion, disconnection, and mistrust. Choosing to forgive doesn't imply that you'll feel happy and lovingly trust the person, nor does it imply that you shouldn't feel any negative emotions.

## Being a Pushover

Since abusers are manipulative and sneaky, it's important to feel both physically and emotionally safe. Forgiveness doesn't mean that you continue to put yourself in unsafe situations. And forgiveness can't even be *discussed* until safety is established.

## Praying More

Another incorrect perception of forgiveness is that it magically happens if we believe in God or go to church more. I remember hearing a well-meaning pastor say, "Well, maybe if you were praying more, then you'd have forgiven him by now." We *do* need to pray that God will help us forgive others, but prayer isn't a magic or instant cure for the damage of abuse. Forgiveness takes time, and it involves a lot of pain. Even if some Christians don't understand that, God does. He'll patiently help you along the way.

## FORGIVENESS IS—

## Deciding Not to Get Personal Revenge

When a person does something wrong, they deserve and need negative consequences. But revenge is different from the appropriate negative consequences we discussed previously. Instead, forgiving means that you're not personally going to make your abuser's life miserable. Anger can be a healthy, appropriate response to injustice, but as the apostle Paul cautions us in Ephesians 4:26, we must not let our anger lead us to sin. Revenge is wrong because retribution is God's job—he alone has the right and the ability to create perfect justice by punishing injustice. So forgiveness is letting go of your right to hurt another person for hurting you.

**DO NOT REPAY ANYONE EVIL FOR EVIL....DO NOT TAKE REVENGE, MY DEAR FRIENDS, BUT LEAVE ROOM FOR GOD'S WRATH....DO NOT BE OVERCOME BY EVIL, BUT OVERCOME EVIL WITH GOOD. (ROMANS 12:17-19, 21)**

This step is possible if you believe that God will eventually bring complete justice. A big part of forgiving people who've committed destructive acts of evil against you is to entrust their punishment to God. Abusers *will* have consequences for what they have done, but you're not to be in charge of that. Notice what strong language the Bible uses to talk about people who hurt children: Matthew 18:6 says, "But if anyone causes one of these little ones who believe in me to sin, it would be better for him to have a large millstone hung around his neck and to be drowned in the depths of the sea." You can forgive even unrepentant, evil abusers by letting go of hatred, bitterness, and a desire for revenge, and you can entrust perfect justice to the God of justice.

**"DON'T MISTREAT WIDOWS OR ORPHANS. IF YOU DO AND THEY CRY OUT TO ME, YOU CAN BE SURE I'LL TAKE THEM MOST SERIOUSLY; I'LL SHOW MY ANGER AND COME RAGING AMONG YOU." (EXODUS 22:22-24 *THE MESSAGE*)**

### Understanding That Your Abuser Is Also a Fellow Human Being Who Needs Healing and Forgiveness from God.

Early on you learned about the cycle of abuse and violence. Abused kids sometimes grow up to abuse their kids. That doesn't make it okay, but it can allow you to have some compassion for your abuser(s). They were once hurting kids themselves, and they have not found healing like you are doing now. So even though you feel angry because that person abused you, you can ask God to give you compassion for him or her as a fellow human being made in God's image.

> Ever since I could remember, I had to go and visit my dad in jail. He was always in and out of my family's life. Having to go see your father behind bars is bad enough, but him not being a part of your life is worse. At the end of this year, things should be back to normal. It will be nice not to have dogs smell us just to visit him. I don't want to take anything away from the man...when he's out, he's always there for us.

And, actually, I do kind of feel for him 'cause his mom died when he was fifteen. But that still doesn't give him a right to do what he does.

My dad: state property until December 2015.

– La Voyde, age fifteen

## Praying for Your Abuser

This is perhaps the hardest part of forgiveness for abuse survivors. You need to remember that we all need God's grace. God hates abuse, and he will punish unrepentant abusers, but God says he takes no pleasure in the destruction of evil people—he wants to see them repent and change and find forgiveness and healing (Ezekiel 18:23). That's the only way the cycle of abuse can really be broken. You may feel like you could never pray for your abuser—especially when that person has never owned the pain he or she has caused you. A good place to start is to ask God to give you his heart for your abuser, for God to help you see your abuser as he does.

Remember earlier we talked about how God loves you and allows you to feel guilt and pain so that you'll turn away from unhealthy, sinful practices. When you pray for your abuser(s), it's good to pray that some day that person will experience enough pain and consequences that he or she would be driven to God, confess, and find healing from the sin that's destroying him or her and others.

Maybe the idea of your abuser(s) completely turning from abusive patterns, confessing sins, being truly remorseful, and owning his or her behavior seems completely impossible. Humanly, it is. But God can and does do this. One of the most incredible examples of a chronic abuser making a complete turnaround is the apostle Paul. In chapter one we talked about how Paul had tortured and even fatally abused Christians. God worked in Paul's heart in a dramatic way, and Paul made a complete turnaround. He confessed his sins and changed the course of his life. He went from being someone who physically abused Christians in the name of his religion to a Christian who was willing to be abused for his faith in Christ.

In Romans, Paul talks about the people who were trying to kill him. He didn't want them to be destroyed by God in judgment, so he prayed they would see the truth and come to God. He had compassion for them as lost people. Romans 9:2; 10:1 says, "I have great sorrow and unceasing anguish in my heart....Brothers, my heart's desire and prayer to God for the Israelites is that they may be saved."

## A Process

Forgiveness is not something you can decide to do once and then it's done. You do need to prayerfully decide to let go of bitterness and ask God to give you his heart for the person who's hurt you. This decision begins the process of forgiveness—but it's not the end of it. When forgiveness involves someone who has hurt you deeply, there will be memories that continue to come out of the blue. When the memory gets triggered again, it's normal for feelings of anger or bitterness to come back up. Every time this happens, you need to continue to ask God to help you and to continue to choose to let go of bitterness and the desire for revenge. As you're consistent with this process, it will get easier to forgive.

C. S. Lewis was a Christian writer who lived in the mid-twentieth century. He's most famous for writing the Chronicles of Narnia. In one of his books, he shares part of his own story and implies that he was sexually abused in boarding school. He wrestled long and hard with the topic of forgiveness. As a mature Christian leader, here's the conclusion he made about forgiving those who have deeply wounded us.

> There is no use in talking as if forgiveness were easy. We all know the old joke, "You've given up smoking once; I've given it up a dozen times." In the same way I could say of a certain man, "Have I forgiven him for what he did that day? I've forgiven him more times than I can count." For we find that the work of forgiveness has to be done over and over again.[2]

## FORGIVENESS MIGHT BE—

### Restoring the Relationship

This can happen only if your abuser takes full responsibility for his abuse, recognizes that it was wrong and harmful, gives solid evidence of having a major change of attitude and behavior, and submits to the appropriate consequences. The Bible calls this *repentance*. Luke 17:3 says, "Watch yourselves. 'If your brother sins, rebuke him, and *if he repents*, forgive him'" [emphasis added]. Jesus is talking here about relational forgiveness. He knows that you offer this kind of forgiveness only when there's repentance. You can, and should, still forgive in the sense of letting go of hatred and bitterness, but to go back into a relationship with that person shouldn't happen unless there's been real repentance.

It's important to note that repentance is not just apologizing. Many times unrepentant abusers apologize in order to convince themselves that they're good people who don't have a serious problem. Real repentance means having a deep change of heart and mind about one's sin and the proven change of behavior to go with it (Matthew 3:8). In order for a turnaround to be sincere, the abuser must experience a noticeable amount of negative emotion. It's not just being sorry about being caught, it's being truly sorry for one's sin and the way those sins dishonored God and hurt other people.

Restoring the relationship is a step that's often inappropriate to take until you're an adult. If your abuser is older than you, then there's an imbalance of power. Once you are an adult and are able to view the abuser as an equal, then it could be okay to restore the relationship.

## So Do You Forgive an Abuser?

This is a tricky question because there are different kinds of forgiveness. Yes, you're to forgive people who've abused you—that is, you should let go of bitterness and hatred and ask God to work in their hearts. This kind of forgiveness pleases God and it frees you. Nursing bitterness toward people who've harmed you ultimately hurts you much more than it hurts them.

In Tyler Perry's play *Madea's Class Reunion*, there's an amazing scene between Madea and a young lady who was in an abusive relationship. Madea gives this advice:

> You've got to forgive people. Your mama, daddy, sister, brother, your ex, your uncle. I don't care what they done did to you. Forgive them folk. Not for them but for you. If you've been raped, beat, hurt, molested…it don't matter what they did…forgive them. You walk around holding all that stuff while they're sleeping at night. 'Oh, I'm going to fix you, I'm going to be mad.' That ain't gonna do nothing but eat at you. There are people dead in the grave that still got a hold on people walking 'round this earth because of something they did to them. Now that's what sad. Let that stuff go. You can't fly with a whole bunch of stuff holding you down.[3]

Relational forgiveness—or reconciliation—is different. This can only happen *after* you've let go of bitterness, had some time to heal, and are an adult. Restoring the relationship can't happen when the abuser is still in a position of authority or control over you. The other concern is to know for certain if the abuser is now a safe person. Remember how abusers tend to trick us? Remember how they can act sorry just to satisfy their own guilt or to manipulate? You'll know an abuser is truly sorry when you see that he's taking full responsibility for the abusive behavior (admitting you were not at fault) and when he's taking clear steps toward healing (going to counseling, turning himself in to the authorities, etc.).

A forgiveness that follows these principles breathes hope into something that is horrifyingly evil. It offers the hope of healing for abuse survivors and a call for abusers to get their acts together.[4]

# Chapter Eleven Activities

## LEVEL ONE

On pages 166–167 read through the list of what forgiveness is not. Have you ever been taught any of these wrong things? Which ones?

Who are the people or what are the situations you feel anger toward? Write down anything that still feels charged with emotion when you think about it. Your list may include yourself and God. Be honest as you write. You don't have to share your whole list.

## LEVEL TWO

Reread the quotation from *Madea's Class Reunion* on page 171. How do you think holding on to anger or resentment affects people? How might your anger and unforgiveness be holding you down?

What reasons do you have for not wanting to forgive?

What reasons do you have for wanting to forgive?

## LEVEL THREE

On a separate sheet of paper, write a letter to God. Be completely honest and unfiltered. Because he loves you, he wants your honest heart—so be completely open and thorough. Don't leave anything out. Pray before you begin, asking God to help you trust this unfiltered process. He'll bring to mind the memories, hurts, and feelings that need to be expressed. So write it all! Then, when you're finished, write your specific requests of God. What do you need most from him? Help with confusion? Reassurances of his presence? Hope for your future? Guidance? Make specific requests of God as you would a close friend. He loves you more than anyone ever will.

Imagine for a moment that God keeps a journal. Write out what you think he would write in his journal about your abuser. Then write what you think he's saying to you.[5]

What do you know about your abuser's childhood? From what you have learned from this book, what might be his or her story? Describe it below.

Think about the people in your life who've hurt you significantly, then write the following: "I forgive _____ for_____ . I'll let God deal with you or punish you for what you've done to me. I'm letting this go and giving it to God. I don't want to be chained to you anymore. I'm going to move on with my life and throw away what you've done and how it has affected me. I'm done with you, and I'm done with my self-protection. I choose to be healthy, happy, and have good relationships with safe people who can meet my needs."

Some people feel a lot of relief after writing letters to symbolize letting go of the anger, hurt, and resentments. Some suggestions:

- Tear the papers into tiny pieces and make a collage of hope and healing, using positive quotes and pictures in addition to the scraps.
- Burn the papers.
- Hike into the woods, desert, or mountains to bury the papers.

I'm sure you can come up with something meaningful to you. Do it now!

Chapter Twelve

# WHERE DO YOU GO FROM HERE?

Well, you've made it to the end of the book! You might be asking, "Where do I go from here?" Before our time together is done, we want to make sure you have some options. We hope that in the process of reading this book, you've taken the time to journal and also begin connecting with other safe people.

## Physical Safety

Your safety is our number one priority. Every state has different hotlines and phone numbers to call if you're in danger. A great national resource is called the National Child Abuse Hotline. They have trained counselors who will be a support for you. You can stay completely anonymous (they won't know who you are unless you tell them), which can make talking easier. They can't take away your control because without your name, they can't call the police or local Child Protection agency. But they may encourage *you* to do that because your safety is *very* important. If you feel unsafe or just need to talk, we encourage you to give them a call. Also, their website is helpful and has more information.

| | | |
|---|---|---|
| Childhelp Child Abuse Hotline | 1-800-4ACHILD www.childhelpusa.org | Provides multilingual crisis intervention and professional counseling on child abuse. Gives referrals to local social service groups offering counseling on child abuse. Has literature on child abuse in English and Spanish. Operates 24 hours. |
| Girls & Boys Town National Hotline | 1-800-448-3000 www.boystown.org www.girlstownfoundation.org | For children and parents in any type of personal crisis. Trained counselors will provide help in abusive relationships, parent-child conflicts, pregnancy, runaway youth, suicide, physical and sexual abuse. Operates 24 hours. |
| National Runaway Hotline | 1-800-231-6946 | Provides information and referral for shelter, counseling, medical and legal services, and transportation back home. Operates a personal, confidential message relay service between runaways and their families. Operates 24 hours. |
| Covenant House Nineline | 1-800-999-9999 | Crisis line for youth, teens, and families. Locally based referrals throughout the United States. Help for youth and parents regarding drugs, abuse, homelessness, runaway children, and message relays. Operates 24 hours. |
| National Youth Crisis Hotline | 1-800-442-HOPE | Provides services for children and youth who are abused, suicidal, chemically dependent, depressed over family or school problems, runaways, or abandoned. Operates 24 hours. |

# Emotional Safety

The next order of business after physical safety is finding safe places to heal. As you work through your history, you'll need the love and support of others, and your friends can be a huge help with that. However, you need to involve someone older and wiser with the bigger stuff. Even though we're adults, we don't limit our advice to only friends our own age. We still ask for the advice of older adults who can give us a different view of things. You can think of these older adults as mentors or relationship coaches. So find a teacher, coach, youth leader, pastor, family member, or some safe adult who's already in your life and can help you with this stuff.

Another great way to get support is to go to a support group. There might be support groups at your school or youth group.

If it fits your situation, you might consider going to a twelve-step meeting. These are meetings that are not necessarily faith-based, and there are millions of meetings throughout the world. The purpose of twelve-step meetings is to offer a spiritual solution to life's problems without requiring adherence to any specific set of beliefs or concept of God. You'll feel very accepted no matter what you believe, and you'll be able to define your higher power in a way that feels comfortable for you. AA (Alcoholics Anonymous), NA (Narcotics Anonymous), and many others have teen meetings.

There are also some churches that offer Christian twelve-step groups for teens. Your pastor or teacher can help you find one of these if you are interested. Here are some websites that will help you find a meeting in your area:

**AA:** http://www.alcoholics-anonymous.org

**NA:** http://www.na.org

## Do You Need Counseling?

If you're interested in seeking professional counseling, the best first step is to talk to a counselor at your school or a youth pastor at your church. They should have some connections in your community and will be able to help get you hooked up. Here's the thing with counseling: It's very likely going to involve your parent or guardian. Typically, counseling costs money and you'll need your parent or guardian's help with that. Also, if you're under eighteen years of age, then most counselors (outside of school) can't see you without parent or guardian permission. Don't let that scare you. A good school counselor or youth leader can help you talk with your parents/guardians and explain what you need. Here's the thing with parents/guardians. They almost all think that their teen/young adult needs counseling anyway since you're so much different than they were as a child. All of that change scares the pants off of them, so it shouldn't be hard to convince them that counseling would be helpful.

A creative approach I (Kristi) use is to ask the parents/guardians to tell me what concerns them about their student. Eventually in our conversation, they come up with the idea of taking their son/daughter to counseling. Then I help them suggest the idea to the student. The parent/guardian never knows that the student wanted counseling in the first place. It works every time. So hopefully you can get someone to help you come up with your own plan. Hey, you gotta do what you gotta do!

Something else about counseling—you're the only one who can decide if a counselor is right for you. It's okay to talk to a counselor on the phone before a session (if he or she refuses, that's a sign to keep looking). Ask questions and see how much experience he or she has in working with abuse and with teens or young adults. Many students say that it bugs them when they go to a counselor who either treats them like a little kid or uses big words they don't understand. You want someone who likes working with teens and young adults, and not everyone can do that well. The other thing is that students frequently say it's annoying when counselors won't talk back or give some advice. Our guess is you don't want to hear a counselor say, "And how does that make you feel?" two hundred times in an hour (and who can blame you?). If you want feedback from the counselor and he or she's not giving it to you, ask. If a counselor doesn't feel safe, go somewhere else. A good counselor will call you out on issues from time to time—which may not always be what you want to hear—but no matter what, you should always feel cared about, heard, respected, and understood. Always.

## Mary's Story

We're going to wrap up our time together by letting you read Mary's story, which was originally told in *Mending the Soul*. It starts out when she was fourteen years old, just entering high school. I hope that you find encouragement and feel challenged through her story.

Mary sobbed uncontrollably on the bathroom floor. Her mother stroked her hair and held her until she could finally speak. Mary's first day of high school had been a…nightmare. She had gotten into a fight with a classmate, had threatened the principal, and was on the verge of being expelled from school…Ever since she entered adolescence Mary had grown increasingly rebellious and withdrawn. The precocious little girl who wore fairy dresses and drew pictures of puppies now wore black and drew pictures of corpses. Mary attempted suicide twice in junior high. In fits of rage she would curse her parents for not aborting her before she was born. Finally Mary began to speak to her mother in barely audible whispers. She told about a boy at school who had threatened her friend. Her cruel classmate had triggered dark memories that she had spent years trying to escape. Finally she could no longer hold back the terrible images. She shamefully recounted that five years earlier, her cousin had sexually molested her over a period of two years while he was babysitting her.[1]

Because of the response of Mary's loving parents, she began to get help and find healing for her abuse. She has since graduated from college and is happily married. Today she's a social worker helping kids from the inner city who are going through hard stuff like she did at one time. Below is a letter written by Mary years after she initially disclosed her abuse.

Healing from abuse has been a long process for me. It didn't happen overnight. The years after my disclosure were the hardest years of my life. I want to remind [you] that healing from abuse takes time, patience, and support from others. It is often "two steps forward and one step backward." I think it's important to remember this and not beat [yourself] up if the process is taking much longer than [you] expected. My healing came very slowly. It started with my parents, who loved me tenaciously. They loved me when I was acting unlovable, and they stuck by my side when I was angry. If possible, [you] should find someone who will love [you] like this. It could be a parent, a sibling, a friend, a pastor, or a counselor. Before [you] can accept and love [yourself], [you] must experience unconditional love from someone else. After I accepted that my parents loved me no matter what, I began to trust other people. I started by telling a close friend about the abuse. I gradually began to trust people in seemingly little ways, such as going on dates with guys or letting more of my true self show to friends. I encourage [you] to open up to people, when [you] feel ready, so [you] can experience trust again. In my journey, I found the more I could trust other people, the more I could trust God.

As an abuse victim, healing my relationship with God has been the hardest thing I've ever done. It took the most time and was the most painful, but eventually it happened. For a long time I was very angry with God. Although I continued going to church, I didn't feel a lot of love for God, and that was okay. During my healing I learned that it's okay to feel angry with God! He even wants us to tell him about this anger. I found it helpful to write letters to God about how confused and angry I was toward him, and to ask him to show himself to me.

I'd like to say again to anyone reading this book who has been abused that deep healing takes time. Please don't rush the process. Pray for God to show you the good he wants to bring out of your abuse. I truly believe that if I can experience healing, anyone can![2]

— Mary

# Conclusion

Thank you for allowing us to take this journey with you. We're proud that you have the strength and courage to begin facing your pain, see how it affects you, and begin to have hope that your future can be filled with joy and freedom. Remember, healing is a process and you'll likely need to read through this book again. Each time you do, you'll dig deeper and heal more completely. There are more *Mending the Soul* resources that have been written for adults that go even deeper than this book, so there will always be opportunities for you to keep healing and growing. Over time the process gets easier and it's very cool that you're starting your process at a young age.

The following quote was made famous at the end of the movie *Coach Carter*. It's an excellent reminder that no matter what pain we have experienced in our past, we can be free to live our lives to their fullest and then help others. We hope that as you experience both pain and victory in your life, you'll never settle for anything less than the best.

> Our deepest fear is not that we are inadequate. Our deepest fear is that we are powerful beyond measure. It is our light, not our darkness, that most frightens us. We ask ourselves, Who am I to be brilliant, gorgeous, talented, and fabulous? Actually, who are you *not* to be? You are a child of God. Your playing small doesn't serve the world. There's nothing enlightened about shrinking so that other people won't feel insecure around you. We are all meant to shine, as children do. We are born to make manifest the glory of God that is within us. It's not just in some of us; it's in everyone. And as we let our own light shine, we unconsciously give other people permission to do the same. As we're liberated from our own fear, our presence automatically liberates others.[3]

# Chapter Twelve Activities

## LEVEL ONE

This book was divided into four parts: Figuring Out Your Pain, When Your Relationships Hurt, When You Hurt, and Healing Your Pain. Look back through the book and choose the three most significant things you learned in each section.

Figuring Out Your Pain:

When Your Relationships Hurt:




When You Hurt:




Healing Your Pain:




## LEVEL TWO
Reflect on your journaling from the first few chapters of this book. What things have changed since you started this process? How have you seen yourself take some risks? How have you grown as a result of this journey?

How do you feel about what you've learned in this book? Take some time to write about your feelings.

How will reading this book impact you in the future? What can you do to make sure that this wasn't just an educational exercise for you, but one that will make a difference in your life?

## LEVEL THREE

Go back through this book and revisit any areas that you skipped. Complete any activities you weren't ready for the first time. Remember, healing is a process, so you'll need to reread this book and take it a little deeper the next time. Then, when you are ready, there's a book and workbook for adults that will help you take your healing to a whole new level.

Finally, make a collage (you can use pictures and/or words) that depicts the place you're in now, as you finish this book. Date it so that you'll always remember what the Lord did for you in this year. When you are finished with the collage, make a copy and put it into the back flap of this book. You'll appreciate looking back at it in the years to come.

# APPENDIX

Feelings

AFRAID · ANGRY · ANXIOUS · ASHAMED · CHEERFUL · CONFUSED

CURIOUS · DEPRESSED · DISAPPOINTED · DISGUSTED · EMBARRASSED · ENCOURAGED

ENRAGED · GLAD · GLOOMY · GRATEFUL · GUILTY · HOPEFUL

HURT · INSECURE · INSIGNIFICANT · INVISIBLE · ISOLATED · JEALOUS

JOYFUL · LONELY · MISERABLE · MISUNDERSTOOD · NERVOUS · OVERWHELMED

PROUD · PUZZLED · REGRETFUL · REJECTED · RESENTFUL · SAD

SHOCKED · UNAPPRECIATED · UNSETTLED · VIOLATED · VULNERABLE · WITHDRAWN

# ENDNOTES

## Introduction

1. All Scripture citations are from the *New International Version* (2011) unless otherwise stated.

## Chapter One

1. Celestia G. Tracy, *Mending the Soul Workbook*, 3rd ed. (Phoenix: Mending the Soul Ministries, 2009), 17–71.

## Chapter Two

1. Steven R. Tracy, *Mending the Soul: Understanding and Healing Abuse* (Grand Rapids: Zondervan, 2005), 29.
2. More specifically, 57 percent of the children who were abused suffered physical abuse. J. Sedlak et al., *Fourth National Incidence Study of Child Abuse and Neglect (NIS–4): Report to Congress, Executive Summary* (Washington, D.C.: U.S. Department of Health and Human Services, Administration for Children and Families, 2010), 6. These figures were based on the Endangerment Standard of child maltreatment.
3. S. Tracy, *Mending the Soul*, 29.
4. L. A. Greenfield et al., *Violence by Intimates: Analysis of Data on Crimes by Current or Former Spouses, Boyfriends, and Girlfriends* (Washington, D.C.: U.S. Department of Justice, 1998); Jacquelyn C. Campbell et al., "Assessing Risk Factors for Intimate Partner Homicide," *National Institute of Justice Journal* 250 (2003): 18.
5. R. M. Bolen and M. Scannapieco, "Prevalence of Child Sexual Abuse: A Corrective Metanalysis," *Social Service Review* 73 (1999): 281–313.

6. Erin A. Casey and Paula S. Nurius, "Trends in the Prevalence and Characteristics of Sexual Violence: A Cohort Analysis," *Violence and Victims* 21 (2006): 629–44.
7. C. Tracy, *Mending the Soul Workbook*, 58.
8. National Committee for the Prevention of Child Abuse. This can be accessed on the Web at *www.safechild.org/childabuse3.htm*.
9. S. Tracy, *Mending the Soul*, 34.
10. Ibid., 32.

## Chapter Three

1. S. Tracy, *Mending the Soul*, 30.
2. Sedlak et al., *Fourth National Incidence Study, Executive Summary*, 6.
3. B. A. van der Kolk, J. C. Perry, and J. L. Herman, "Childhood Origins of Self-Destructive Behavior," *American Journal of Psychiatry* 148 (1991): 1665–71.
4. A. L. Miller, J. H. Rathus, and M. M. Linehan, *Dialectical Behavior Therapy for Suicidal Adolescents*. (New York: Guilford Press, 2007).
5. C. Tracy, *Mending the Soul Workbook*, 57.

## Chapter Four

1. Alecia Moore (P!nk) and Scott Storch, "Family Portrait," *M!ssundaztood*, Artista Records, 2001.
2. Sheryl A. Benton and Dorinda J. Lambert, Kansas State University Counseling Services; can be accessed on the Web at *www.k-state.edu/counseling/topics/relationships/dysfunc.html*.
3. S. Tracy, *Mending the Soul*, 38–48.
4. C. Tracy, *Mending the Soul Workbook*, 111.

## Chapter Five

1. Jay G. Silverman et al., "Dating Violence Against Adolescent Girls and Associated Substance Abuse, Unhealthy Weight Control, Sexual Risk Behavior, Pregnancy, and Suicidality," *Journal of the American Medical Association* 286 (2001): 572–79.
2. "Liz Claiborne Inc. Omnibuzz® Topline Findings: Teen Relationship Abuse Research"; can be accessed on the Web at *www.teenresearch.com*.
3. "Tween and Teen Dating Violence and Abuse Study," Teenage Research Unlimited for Liz Claiborne Inc. and the National Teen Dating Abuse Helpline, February 2008; can be accessed on the Web at *www.loveisnotabuse.com*.
4. S. Tracy, *Mending the Soul*, 213–16.

5. Gene Edward Veith, "Sex and the Evangelical Teen," *World Magazine*, August 11, 2007, 9. This article is reporting on the work of sociologist Mark Regnerus, *Forbidden Fruit: Sex and Religion in the Lives of American Teenagers* (New York: Oxford University Press, 2007).

6. "Survey Shows Faith Impacts Some Behaviors but Not Others," *The Barna Update*, October 22, 2002; can be accessed on the Web at *www.barna.org/barna-update/article/5-barna-update/83-survey-shows-faith-impacts-some-behaviors-but-not-others.*

7. One Barna study found that among adults who have been married, born again Christians and non-Christians have essentially the same probability of divorce (about 33 percent). "The Year's Most Intriguing Findings from Barna Research Studies," *The Barna Update*, December 17, 2001; can be accessed on the Web at *www.barna.org/barna-update/article/5-barna-update/64-the-years-most-intriguing-findings-from-barna-research-studies.*

8. Jessica Bennett, "The Pornification of a Generation," *Newsweek*, October 7, 2008.

9. Jane D. Brown and Kelly L. L'Engle, "X-Rated: Sexual Attitudes and Behaviors Associated With U.S. Early Adolescents' Exposure to Sexually Explicit Media," *Communication Research* 36 (2009): 129–51.

10. James V. P. Check and Ted H. Guloien, "Reported Proclivity for Coercive Sex Following Repeated Exposure to Sexually Violent Pornography, Nonviolent Dehumanizing Pornography, and Erotica," in *Pornography Research Advances and Policy Considerations*, ed. Dolf Zillmann and Jennings Bryant (Hillsdale, N.J.: Lawrence Erlbaum, 1989), 170–71.

11. Doug McKenzie-Mohr and Mark P. Zanna, "Treating Women as Sexual Objects: Look to the (Gender Schematic) Male Who Has Viewed Pornography," *Personality and Social Psychology Bulletin* 16 (1990): 296–308.

12. *Special Report: Violence Among Family Members and Intimate Partners* (Washington, D.C.: Federal Bureau of Investigation, rev. January 2005), 344.

13. J. C. Straton, "The Myth of the 'Battered Husband Syndrome,'" *Masculinities* 2 (1994): 79–82.

14. Karen M. Wilson and Jonathan D. Klein, "Opportunities for Appropriate Care: Health Care and Contraceptive Use Among Adolescents Reporting Unwanted Sexual Intercourse," *Archives of Pediatrics and Adolescent Medicine* 156 (2002): 341–4.

15. For a development of the biblical teaching on premarital sexual abstinence and social science research supporting this, see Steven R.

Tracy, "Chastity and the Goodness of God: The Case for Premarital Sexual Abstinence," *Themelios* 31 (2006): 54–71.

16. Ibid., 66

# Chapter Six

1. Howard N. Snyder and Melissa Sickmund, *Juvenile Offenders and Victims: 2006 National Report* (Washington D.C.: U.S. Department of Justice, Office of Juvenile Justice and Delinquency Prevention, 2006).

2. D. K. Eaton et al., "Youth Risk Behavior Surveillance—United States, 2009," *Morbidity and Mortality Weekly Report* 59, June 4, 2010; can be accessed on the Web at www.cdc.gov/mmwr.

3. Snyder and Sickmund, *Juvenile Offenders and Victims: 2006 National Report*.

4. Ibid.

5. B. A. van der Kolk, J. C. Perry, and J. L. Herman, "Childhood Origins of Self-Destructive Behavior," *American Journal of Psychiatry* 148 (1991): 1669.

6. Barbara Owen and Barbara Bloom, "Profiling the Needs of Young Female Offenders," in *A Report to the Executive Staff of the California Youth Authority*, July 1997, 8.

7. Catherine Stevens-Simon and Susan Reichert, "Sexual Abuse, Adolescent Pregnancy, and Child Abuse: A Developmental Approach to an Intergenerational Cycle," *Archives of Pediatrics and Adolescent Medicine* 148 (1994): 23–27.

8. R. Campbell et al., "The Relationship between Adult Sexual Assault and Prostitution: An Exploratory Analysis," *Violence and Victims* 18 (2003): 299–317.

9. Elisabeth Simantov, Cathy Schoen, and Jonathan D. Klein, "Health-Compromising Behaviors: Why Do Adolescents Smoke or Drink? Identifying Underlying Risk and Protective Factors," *Archives of Pediatrics and Adolescent Medicine* 154 (2000): 1025–33.

10. Dianne Neumark-Sztainer et al., "Disordered Eating Among Adolescents: Associations with Sexual/Physical Abuse and Other Familial/Psychosocial Factors," *International Journal of Eating Disorders* 28 (2000): 249–58.

11. R. F. Anda et al., "The Enduring Effects of Abuse and Related Adverse Experiences in Childhood," *European Archives of Psychiatry and Clinical Neuroscience* 256 (2006): 174–86; Terry Diamond and Robert T. Muller, "The Relationship Between Witnessing Parental Conflict During Childhood and Later Psychological Adjustment Among University Students: Disentangling Confounding Risk Factors," *Canadian Journal of Behavioural Science* 36 (2004): 295–309.

## Chapter Seven

1. S. Tracy, *Mending the Soul*, 74.
2. Christina Aguilera and Linda Perry, "I'm OK," *Stripped*, RCA Records, 2002.

## Chapter Eight

1. Dan B. Allender, *The Wounded Heart: Hope for Adult Victims of Childhood Sexual Abuse*, rev. ed. (Colorado Springs, CO: NavPress, 1995), 114.
2. *Garden State*, Directed by Zach Braff, Fox Searchlight Pictures and Miramax Films, 2004.

## Chapter Nine

1. Kelly Clarkson, David Hodges, and Ben Moody, "Because of You," *Breakaway*, RCA Records, 2004.
2. This quotation is taken from Kelly Clarkson's official website: *http://www.kellyclarkson.com/main.php?content=biography.*
3. Linkin Park, "Easier to Run," *Meteora*, Warner Bros. Records, 2003.
4. P. E. Mullen et al., "The Long-Term Impact of the Physical, Emotional, and Sexual Abuse of Children: A Community Study," *Child Abuse and Neglect* 20 (1996): 7–21.

## Chapter Ten

1. Mike Donehey, Jason Ingram, and Jeff Owen (Tenth Avenue North), "Healing Begins," *The Light Meets the Dark*, Provident, 2010.
2. S. Tracy, *Mending the Soul*, 141.
3. *Child Maltreatment 2004* (Washington, D.C.: U.S. Department of Health and Human Services, Administration on Children, Youth and Families, 2006).
4. S. Tracy, *Mending the Soul*, 146–7.
5. Henri Nouwen, *Life of the Beloved: Spiritual Living in a Secular World* (New York: Crossroad, 1992), 57, 59.

## Chapter Eleven

1. Billie Joe Armstrong, Frank E. Wright III, Michael Pritchard, (Green Day), "Jesus of Suburbia," *American Idiot*, Reprise Records, 2004.
2. C. S. Lewis, *Reflections on the Psalms* (New York: Harcourt, Brace, and World, 1958), 24–25.
3. *Madea's Class Reunion*, The Tyler Perry Collection, Lions Gate, 2005.
4. Paraphrased from S. Tracy, *Mending the Soul*, 194.
5. C. Tracy, *Mending the Soul Workbook*, 223.

# Chapter Twelve

1. S. Tracy, *Mending the Soul*, 11–12.
2. Adapted from S. Tracy, *Mending the Soul*, 195–7.
3. Marianne Williamson, *A Return to Love: Reflections on the Principles of "A Course in Miracles"* (New York: Harper Paperbacks, 1996), 190–91.

Printed in the USA
CPSIA information can be obtained
at www.ICGtesting.com
JSHW031144150724
66428JS00008B/76

9 780310 671435

9 780310 671435